HANDCRAFTED BICYCLES

Richard SACHS
RICHARD S
challenge
STRADA
T38 LITE
RICHARD
SACHS
super record
COLE

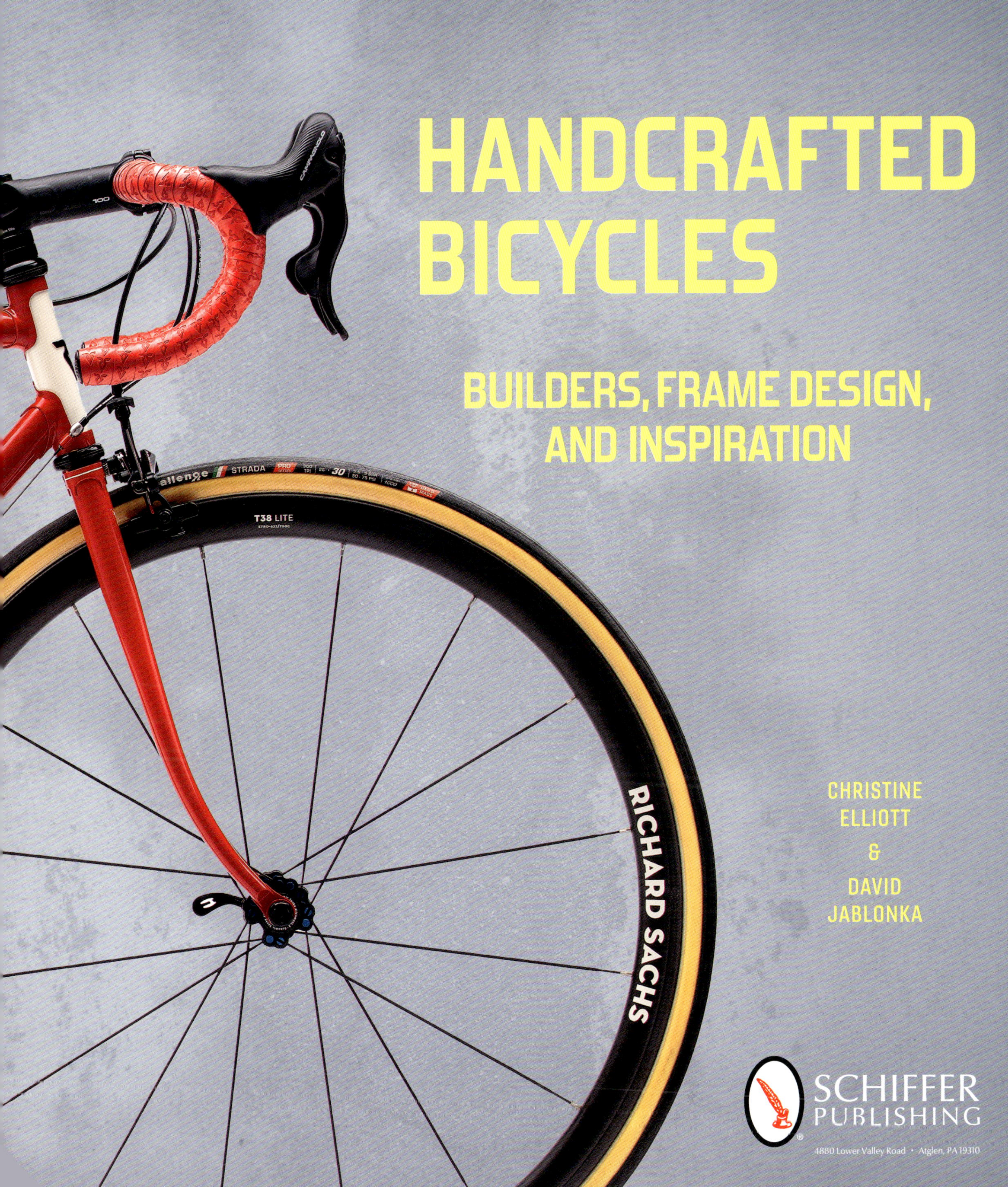

HANDCRAFTED BICYCLES

BUILDERS, FRAME DESIGN, AND INSPIRATION

CHRISTINE ELLIOTT
&
DAVID JABLONKA

SCHIFFER PUBLISHING
4880 Lower Valley Road • Atglen, PA 19310

Front Cover: A Richard Sachs *Simplicity* model frame assembled with Campagnolo S.R. components, COLE - RS wheels, Challenge Strada 30 mm tubular tires, Selle San Marco Aspide saddle, and Deda Elementi seat post, stem, and handlebars. Courtesy of Bruno Ratensperger.

Library of Congress Control Number: 2025930107

Designed by Molly Shields
Type set in Gineso/Cambria

ISBN: 978-0-7643-6974-2
ePub: 978-1-5073-0598-0

Printed in China
Published by Schiffer Publishing, Ltd.

4880 Lower Valley Road
Atglen, PA 19310
Phone: (610) 593-1777; Fax: (610) 593-2002
Email: info@schifferbooks.com
Web: www.schifferbooks.com

For our complete selection of fine books on this and related subjects, please visit our website at www.schifferbooks.com. You may also write for a free catalog. Schiffer Publishing's titles are available at special discounts for bulk purchases for sales promotions or premiums. Special editions, including personalized covers, corporate imprints, and excerpts, can be created in large quantities for special needs. For more information, contact the publisher.

EPIGRAPH

A bicycle hides nothing and threatens nothing. It is what it does, its form is its function.

—Stewart Parker, Irish playwright, Spokesong (1975)

Every time you miss your childhood, ride on a bicycle.

—Mehmet Murat İldan, Turkish playwright and novelist

Everyone in their life has his own particular way of expressing life's purpose—the lawyer his eloquence, the painter his palette, and the man of letters his pen from which the quick words of his story flow. I have my bicycle.

—Gino Bartali, Italian champion cyclist

CONTENTS

ACKNOWLEDGMENTS

A huge thank-you to the thirty-two bicycle builders and bicycle-building teams who accepted our invitation to be featured in *Handcrafted Bicycles: Builders, Frame Design, and Inspiration*. We appreciate you all for taking time away from your busy schedules to correspond with us, provide spectacular photos, answer our questions, from which the narrative for each chapter has been created, and for sending all other supporting documents. Thank you to the following:

Zach Geller of Acoustic Cycles; Joseph Ahearne of Ahearne Cycles; Javier Valiente of Amapola Cycles; Erik Bergstrom and Argonaut team of Argonaut Cycles; Quentin Polizzi of Atelier des Vélos; Darren Baum and Matt Wikstrom of Baum Cycles; Driss Boucif of BCB; Stephen Bilenky of Bilenky Cycle Works; Craig Calfee of Calfee Design; Olivier Csuka of Cycles Alex Singer; Ikuo Tsuchiya of Cycles Grand Bois; Cristina Würdig, Pietro Pietricola, and Pegoretti team of Dario Pegoretti; David Wages of Ellis Cycles; Florian Haeussler of Fern Bicycles; James Buckley of Finnbar Trout Cycles; Chris Besnia of Goodday Bikeworks; Ralf Holleis of Huhn Cycles; Fabio Putzolu of ICHNU Cycles; Steven Harvey and Dan Farrell of Moulton Bicycle Company; Sam Whittingham of Naked Bicycles and Design; Bob Parlee and Tom Rodi of Parlee Cycles; Mark and Kelly Hester of Prova Cycles; Robert Quirk of Quirk Cycles; Richard Sachs of Richard Sachs Cycles; Rubén Durán of Rizzo Cycles; Santiago Tora of Scarab Cycles; Danielle Schön of Schön Studio; Stefan Sueess of SUEESS Frameworks; Jeremy Sycip of Sycip Designs; Chris Yeomans of TJ Cycles; Barbara Tommasini and the Tommasini team of Tommasini; and Arnaud Pornin of Woodalps.

This is a broad but not exhaustive list of bicycle builders. Many builders worthy of inclusion were contacted but for various reasons were not able to participate.

Thank you also to the bike builders' photographers, who are credited with providing spectacular photos for the book. They are:

Alexandra Demopoulos, Alexandra Demopoulos Photos; Zach Geller, Robert Huff—Bob Huff Photo, and Katie Sox—Katie Sox Photography for Acoustic Cycles; Joseph Ahearne, Christopher Igleheart, Billy Sinkford, and Dylan VanWeelden for Ahearne Cycles; Amapola Cycles for Amapola Cycles; Argonaut Cycles for Argonaut Cycles; Léandre Chéron and Crea Lens Film for Atelier des Vélos; Spurlo Style Photography for Baum Cycles; Chipo Sikumba and Adam Gasson for BCB; Bilenky Cycle Works, Daniel Maloney, Nick McCormick, *Philadelphia Magazine*, Brad Quartuccio, and Conor Urian for Bilenky Cycle Works; Drew Rogers for Calfee Design; Ernest Benoit-Ourion—Cyclopast, Christian Bille, Walter Csuka, Cycles Alex Singer, and Gabriel Refait for Cycles Alex Singer; Cycles Grand Bois for Cycles Grand Bois; Aaron Guy Leroux—rights by Officina Dario Pegoretti, and Officina Dario Pegoretti for Dario Pegoretti; Peter DiAntoni, Chris Harris, Drew Triplett, David Wages, and Deborah Wages for Ellis Cycles; Stefan Haehnel for Fern Bicycles; James Buckley, Adam Gasson, and Johannes Herden for Finnbar Trout Cycles; Miles Arbor, Neil Beltchenko, Chris Besnia, Arly Landry, Tory Power, and John Watson for Goodday Bikeworks; Pietro Borra, Ralf Holleis Dipl. Industrial Designer, Lars Scharl, and Jörg Spaniol for Huhn Cycles; Adam Gasson and Fabio Putzolu for ICHNU Cycles; Dan Farrell, George Llewellyn, and Robert Smith for Moulton Bicycle Company; Kari Medig and Naked Bicycles and Design for Naked Bicycles and Design; Hunter Kelley and Parlee Cycles, Inc., for Parlee Cycles; Mason Hender, Dave Rome, Erik Son, John Watson—The Radavist, Josh Weinberg—The Radavist, and Andy White for Prova Cycles;

Nikoo Hamzavi, photographer for Quirk Cycles; Richard Sachs, Brian Vernor, and Bruno Ratensperger for Richard Sachs Cycles; @athleticaffair, @huffy808foto, @dylanvanweelden, Rocío María Morales Alvarez, Nil Camarasa—The Service Course, Ale Cubino, Enve Composites, Victor Merino—Sanferbike, and Gianfranco Tripodo for Rizzo Cycles; Enve Composites, MADE Bike Show—@huffy808foto, and @ dylanvanweelden, David Jaramillo—A-Burra entre Montañas; Nicolás Muñoz, and Scarab Cycles for Scarab Cycles; Jarrod A Bunk, Danielle Schön, Pat Valade—The Radavist, and Josh Weinberg—The Radavist for Schön Studio; Gae2tan Bally—Keystone, and SUEESS Frameworks for SUEESS Frameworks; Erik Fenner—Chris King Components, Sycip Designs, John Watson, and Chris Wells for Sycip Designs; Jim Holland—Instagram@j.h.o.l.l.a.n.d, Sabina Kinghorn, Marcel Le Bachelet—www.mkjlb.co.uk, Frank Valentin, Rae Wilding—www.raewilding.com, and Chris Yeomans for TJ Cycles; Alessandro Baglioni, Fotografia BF—Grosseto, Oliver Soulas, Barbara Tommasini, Tommasini, and Tommasini family for Tommasini; and Arnaud Pornin for Woodalps.

Thank you to Val Nagle for sourcing bicycle quotes for the Epigraph. Val has been a presenter of the Yarra Bicycle Users Group Radio show on 3CR Community Radio in Melbourne, Australia, since 2008. Val, your contribution to *Handcrafted Bicycles: Builders, Frame Design, and Inspiration* is very much appreciated.

A special thank you to Joe Boschetti, publishing and media agent, Boschetti Books, for introducing us to Peter Schiffer, managing director of Schiffer Publishing. He played a crucial role in coordinating and leading a conversation to discuss the concept of a new bicycle book. Thank you also, Joe, for your support throughout this project. Your feedback is always valued and much appreciated.

Thank you, Peter Schiffer and the Schiffer team, for bringing *Handcrafted Bicycles: Builders, Frame Design, and Inspiration* to fruition.

INTRODUCTION

Handcrafted Bicycles: Builders, Frame Design, and Inspiration celebrates the bicycle form through the creative and skilled work of thirty-two bicycle builders from thirteen countries—Australia, Belgium, Canada, Colombia, France, Germany, Italy, Japan, Netherlands, Spain, Switzerland, the UK, and the US. Their photographers have captured them in their workshops, close-up details of bike features, completed bikes, and action shots taken in various locations around the world.

The alphabetically arranged chapters comprise spectacular photos, which heroize the builders' artisanship, and the accompanying text offers a window into their backgrounds, techniques, design influences, and viewpoints, with interesting anecdotes along the way. Their responses to our questions about bikes, brand history, workspace, techniques, design theories, inspiration, customer stories, and other life activities emanate from an interesting mix of circumstantial, cultural, and philosophical influences.

To quote Stefan Sueess, one of the featured bike builders: "A bicycle is simply two frame triangles joined together. It's that simple." Or as Richard Hallett, author of *The Bike Deconstructed*, puts it, "A metal frame, two wheels, pedals, a seat, and handlebars—on first glance, bicycles look pretty straightforward."[1] Yet, it is *this* simplicity that makes the bicycle's form and function so iconic. Furthermore, American architect Louis Henry Sullivan's famous expression "Form follows function" is often referred to as a guiding principle for the builders throughout this book.[2]

According to *The Wright Brothers* author David McCullough, the modern bicycle emerged from the so-called safety bike, which had two wheels of the same size and sat nearer to the ground. The safety bike was developed in response to the "high wheelers" of the 1870s and '80s, such as the penny-farthing, which were somewhat precarious to ride and challenging to mount and dismount.[3] Moreover, Alex Newton, author of *Bicycles That Changed the World*, explains, "With this single innovation the modern bicycle was born. Almost every bicycle designed since has used mechanical and engineering principles derived from the safety bicycle."[4] This ubiquitous moving object, with its design and function characteristics, is immediately recognizable to the amateur observer.

Aside from the development of the safety bicycle, which Thomas Ambrose notes "was mainly the preserve of rich men of leisure,"[5] various design interpretations of the bicycle frame, too numerous to cover here, were developed in response to emerging markets. To mention a few: step-through or open frames were developed as more women began participating in cycling, while also challenging societal expectations and conventions in the 1880s. In *The History of Cycling in 50 Bikes*, Ambrose points to the Elswick Cycle Company, which he says were "quick to capitalise on this new market with such bicycles as a ladies' version of their Elswick Sports." This bicycle frame not only accommodated voluminous period clothing but afforded women a newfound freedom of movement.[6] A further development occurred around 1886, with the appearance of the tandem bicycle, which gained popularity because it "allowed a lady and gentleman to share a ride together."[7] One could argue that these developments, derived from the safety bike, paved the way for the democratization of cycling. In time, it allowed a broader stratum of society to enjoy greater economic participation, personal transport, travel, and leisure. Another noteworthy evolution from the '60s was the small-wheel bicycle, such as the ones that Moulton Bicycle Company produce. Their first bike, the M1 "F-frame," produced in 1962, featured a small rubber suspension system. According to Newton, this bike "chimed perfectly with the prevailing mood of the 'swinging sixties.'" Its success created quite a stir, and other manufacturers began producing their own small-wheeled versions.[8] As a sidenote, the Museum of Modern Art (MoMA), in New York City, has an Alex Moulton AM2 Bicycle 1983 in their permanent collection, Department of Architecture and Design.[9]

Of the two Wright brothers, McCullough states that "Orville loved bicycles the most. As an admirer who knew him in later years would say, 'Bring up the subject of the shapes of handlebars or types of pedals of early 'safety bicycles' and his whole face lights up.'"[10] As each chapter will reveal, the essence of Orville's reaction to bicycles can be found in the heart and soul of each featured bike builder. Their visceral love for creating beautifully crafted bicycles, through their interpretations of the bicycle frame, components, accessories, and unique design features, is something to revere in an instant-gratification consumer world. This, in turn, is reflected back to them when their customers see and ride their new bicycle for the first time. The excitement of seeing their dream bike become a reality through collaboration and artisanship lights up the faces of customer and builder alike.

The thirty-two bicycle builders featured in this book inevitably bring a vast array of experience to bike building, with regeneration being part of that cycle. Whether they regard it as a trade, profession, artistry, craftsmanship, or fabrication, it is important to recognize the intrinsic reality of the continuum of experience among these bicycle builders. For example, Olivier Csuka of Cycles Alex Singer, established in 1938, continues to build in the tradition of Alex Singer, as did Olivier's father, Ernest, before him. The long-standing history and knowledge held by the likes of Cycles Alex Singer and other cycle brands established in the '50s, '60s, '70s, '80s, '90s and early to mid-2000s is the culmination of years of observing, learning, honing, and executing their acquired skill sets over and over again. With almost five decades of bicycle making "under his torch," featured bike builder Richard Sachs gracefully puts it this way: "I didn't want to be a bicycle maker; I became one." As for the more recent bike-building devotees, with some making the leap to full-time building due to the COVID-19 pandemic, they bring with them a range of skills and years of experience from different industries and professions, such as engineering, blacksmithing, fashion, and art, to name a few.

Whether these thirty-two bicycle builders design and create commuting, road, racing, track, mountain, gravel, randonneur (or long-distance), touring, tandem, cargo, children's bikes, etc.; from steel, aluminum, titanium, carbon, bamboo, wood, or a mix of materials; using traditional tools and machinery or more-modern processes such as 3-D printing, there is a common theme connecting each builder—a special bond forged with bikes in their childhood.

—Christine Elliott and David Jablonka

KRYPTOTAL
ACOUSTIC CYCLES
ROCK SHOX
Continental

ACOUSTIC CYCLES

PINE, COLORADO, US

"Bikes are the ultimate self-powered dichotomy," says Acoustic Cycles owner Zach Geller. When he wants to escape from people, he turns to bikes. Likewise, they are his medium of choice when catching up with a friend: "Bikes are what I use to clear my head, but also what I obsess over before falling asleep. They are what I use to get exercise, but also the excuse for a big postride meal and drink. Bikes can present a real struggle as you ascend that never-ending climb, but then can allow you to feel carefree when bombing down the hard-earned descent."

Zach's bicycle journey started with his father. He says, "I grew up in Colorado Springs with an incredible riding scene. My dad and I would ride the local trails every weekend, which progressed into me dragging him to the bike parks up in the mountains." Zach eventually found himself working in local bike shops during high school and college. After college he continued working part-time in bike shops, "to mostly maintain some industry perks." After observing the regular cycle of people trading in last season's bike for the new improved model, Zach thought, "Wouldn't it be great to have a handmade bike that was built custom for me, could keep up with the ever-changing trends of the bike industry, and would last for years?" From this point, he vowed to learn frame building and wouldn't ride another bike unless it came from his own shop.

Version 2, prototype—steel, high pivot, full-suspension. All handmade in Pine, Colorado. *Courtesy of Robert Huff (Bob Huff Photo)*

Keep it high and tight—Version 2, prototype.
Courtesy of Robert Huff (Bob Huff Photo)

Zach's engineering qualifications initially led him to a career in the commercial construction industry, but, as he says, "My real passion always lay with bikes." His bike-frame-building career started in 2018. At first, he built frames in his spare time until eventually deciding to branch out on his own: "I needed to try something that allowed me to work with my hands, made me truly happy, and allowed for more time with my beautiful family." Although it was a big leap to leave a corporate job with a secure paycheck, he recognized that time and happiness are important things that can't be bought. Acoustic Cycles was born in 2019 with the aim of bringing high-quality, handmade, custom Colorado-produced frames to the bicycling community.

Living, working, and growing up in Colorado has had and continues to have a tremendous impact on the bikes Zach builds: "When the trails turn to dirt and the tires get a little knobbier, that's where my focus lies, and I am certainly influenced by this outdoor playground that I live and work in." Zach brings this passion and knowledge to all off-road bike disciplines, from downhill to gravel, bikepacking to trail riding. Simply put, he likes to build bikes for the type of riding he enjoys. His bikes are heavily influenced by nature—simple, flowing lines that strike a balance between form and function. Zach says, "I like to incorporate a lot of earth tones in our frame finishes but still encourage bright pops of color." For example, a "Colorado Mountain Ball Cactus with its sharp contrast of a bright-pink flower on top of a light-pastel-green body."

Zach's bike-building goal is a perfect-fitting frame, both in function and aesthetics. "I strive to have a client engaged in their frame from conception to hand-off, to ensure they have a real bond with our creation," he says. His goal is to use as many domestic parts and pieces of a bike as possible, and he likes to point to each piece of raw material and each part to know exactly where it came from. The real satisfaction comes when he receives an email or text from an ecstatic customer who loves the way their bike fits, rides, and looks. He says, "This is the 'WHY' when I think about building bicycles." It is a great experience to also receive admiration for our show bikes when exhibiting at bike shows. Zach recalls a lovely interaction with an attendee, while exhibiting at a Handmade Bike Show in Portland, Oregon. He says, "At one point a younger teen bashfully approached me and introduced himself. He said he had been following my journey as a builder for a few years now and had been inspired to learn the profession himself. He was especially interested in the full-suspension bikes I brought along to the show, and hoped one day he could also make his own dual-suspension frame. Personally, I still view myself as a newcomer to the frame-building occupation, and I was shocked that I could inspire someone to want to jump into this vocation. I profoundly thanked the kid for his kind words and gave him a stack of stickers, trying to hide the huge smile he had put on my face." Zach points out that being a small business owner is extremely difficult and taxing, no matter which industry you're in. "That shy teenager probably had no idea, but he helped reinforce the thought that I'm right where I'm supposed to be, passionately making bikes for people looking to escape to nature."

Zach feels lucky to be living and working on a 5-acre property in the mountains southwest of Denver, Colorado, where his 1,000-square-foot workshop houses his tools, equipment, and materials. He's especially fond of his 1950s Bridgeport vertical mill and Power Kraft lathe. As Zach points out, "These tools are crucial for mitering all the tubing and creating smaller brazed and welded-on pieces that adorn each frame. I like to think that using tools that have so much history adds something to each custom frame we produce."

Zach is mostly a solo frame builder, and his wife, a metalsmith, is the chief head badge maker, who works out of her shop space adjacent to his. As Zach says, "With both working from home, it allows us to care for our mountain kiddo." They also share their workspace with the barn cat, Pedals, who watches over the shop at night and the two shop dogs, Mason and Dylan. Zach says, "The shop dogs mostly nap, but I like to think they are cheering me on as I build." Their zoo family, as Zach describes it, also includes two goats.

When not building bikes, Zach spends time with the family exploring their local mountain towns and showing their little one what nature has to offer. Of course, there's always the call of his bikes, and so he tries to sneak out for as many bike rides as he can. And why wouldn't he? As he says, "Living right on the Colorado Trail, I have access to hundreds of miles of trail literally from our back door."

Start 'em young—Custom steel kid's balance bike. *Courtesy of Alexandra Demopoulos (Alexandra Demopoulos Photos)*

Gotta be fast to ride this bright prototype—steel, high pivot, full-suspension bike. *Courtesy of Alexandra Demopoulos (Alexandra Demopoulos Photos)*

Custom steel Fatbike with retro-inspired splatter / fade paint job. *Courtesy of Alexandra Demopoulos (Alexandra Demopoulos Photos)*

Version 2, prototype, in the concrete jungle. *Courtesy of Katie Sox (Katie Sox Photography)*

Custom steel Fatbike with topography-inspired, custom-made frame bag. *Courtesy of Alexandra Demopoulos (Alexandra Demopoulos Photos)*

Custom steel gravel bike—not your typical beach cruiser. *Courtesy of Zach Geller*

Custom steel 29er frame for a local customer. *Courtesy of Alexandra Demopoulos (Alexandra Demopoulos Photos)*

A peak behind the curtain—custom steel frame before finishing. *Courtesy of Zach Geller*

AHEARNE CYCLES

PORTLAND, OREGON, US

Joseph Ahearne is attracted to bikes for all the obvious reasons: freedom, fun, health, for the environment, and engagement with his city and the seasons. Besides, driving in town is one of his least favorite things to do. Joseph puts it this way: "I've been riding in Portland for so long, I think I've got a map of it burned into my brain. It's a good city for riding because it's not too big, and most of the neighborhoods are linked together so you can usually take back roads to get places. Not to mention the city pays attention to the cycling infrastructure and puts money towards it. It could be way better, and safer, but compared to most cities in the US, it's much better for riding. The mild climate helps too. Months of rain can get tiresome, but at least you can still ride. It's hard for me to imagine living someplace where I'd have to drive everyday to make it work. Cycling is so much a part of the quality of my life, and I feel very lucky to be in the place I am, and in a position where I can ride. Biking and walking, just being outside, it's so important to me. It all kind of starts from here—quality of life."

Ahearne Cycles began in 2002, after Joseph took a bike-building class with Tim Paterek, an old-school bike builder and author of the *Paterek Manual* for bicycle frame builders. During the course, conducted out of his garage in Vancouver, Washington, Tim mentioned that he was retiring and selling off his equipment. Joseph seized the opportunity, bought Tim's equipment, and moved it into the garage where he was living. At the time, he was working in a bike shop but soon found himself making bikes and custom racks on his days off. In due course, he offered his coworkers a deal: he'd build them a frame for the cost of the materials. With the $150 to $200 they provided, he bought tubes and dropouts and made a frame. As he explains, "This was early days; I hadn't settled on a brand name and couldn't afford to send bikes to a professional painter, so I'd rattle-can them." He recalls building a bunch of bikes for coworkers, of whom he's sure none would still be on the road. "There's a learning curve, for sure, and the best way to learn is to make every possible mistake, which I did."

Eventually, he did figure things out. Although his handmade racks were hard work, he was determined. Importantly, he got a couple of lucky breaks. His racks and flask holder went to Interbike, an annual bike industry gathering in North America, which put him on the map. Over the next few years, he made a lot of racks, which really taught him how to braze. Joseph says, "Bike orders gradually picked up as well, and with a lot of twists and turns I ended up here, twenty years in it. It's hard to believe."

These days, he works mostly alone apart from some collaborations. Early on he had a couple of employees but quickly learned that managing staff wasn't his strongpoint: "I had a problem with authority, and so putting myself into that role felt hypocritical and just icky. I liked making things, getting my hands dirty, and didn't want to pay attention to the rest." Joseph collaborates with people on certain projects, or parts of the process, but still does his part alone.

Brazing a seat cluster. *Courtesy of Christopher Igleheart*

His collaborative frame-builds come under the name Page Street Cycles, which he uses for small-batch production. Page Street started with his old shop mate, Christopher Igleheart of Igleheart Custom Frames and Forks, who retired to France in 2022.

What about a favorite tool, bike part, technique, or design theory? Tool: Joseph favors his belt grinder because of its versatility. Technique: in general, brazing, either with brass or silver. "I love building fillets and using heat to direct the flow of molten metal," he says. Design theory: function before fashion. In the early years of building bikes, he was chasing styles of bikes— "Fixed gears because they were hip and 29er mountain bikes before they were mass market because they were so fun to ride, and people wanted them." He admits that his biggest design influence has always been the bike he rides. Whenever he rides a bike, there's always a part of his brain paying attention to the ride quality and specific functionality, especially if he's commuting or touring. There are so many possible attributes and adjustments to work with, so he's always refining his ideas. For the first twelve or fifteen years of his career, he made a new bike for himself every year, sometimes every few months. Joseph says, "It was how I learned what I liked and what I wanted. I took a batch of ideas and made them into a bike and rode the hell out of it." He then took the best from that bike and made the next, and so on. If he didn't break the frame, he would sell it to help pay for parts and materials for the next one. "I'm not precious about my bikes. I may love a bike, but it's still always a tool. When I've got a better tool, I'm always ready to let go of the old one. It's like books—you want people to read them, not to let them sit around getting dusty."

Rack installation. *Courtesy of Christopher Igleheart*

There are many satisfying aspects to building bikes: creating the design, the building process, selecting the paintwork, the completed bike, and, of course, handing it over to a happy customer. Joseph says, "Each project has different challenges. Generally, though, I love it when I've gotten to a certain point in the build, and I can stick the fork in the frame and the wheels in it and step back and see what I've got. And then again toward the end, after paint and when hanging all the parts on the bike, seeing for the first time how the vision that has been there for months comes together. It's gratifying when a customer can come pick up their bike in person. Setting the seat height and watching them take a bike for its first ride, seeing them light up, that's about the best thing." He's always amazed when people send him bike photos of them riding their Ahearne or Page Street touring bikes in far-out places such as Vietnam, Nepal, New Zealand, Puerto Rico, Mexico, and Alaska. "It's cool to know they're out there doing it and having a good time, using something I made with my hands in my workshop here. It reminds me I'm connected to people and places in ways that for the most part I don't even know."

Joseph acknowledges that finding a passion for building bikes saved his life. Struggling to find his place in the world, for over twelve years he traveled and did all kinds of

Polished stainless-steel bicycle and flask.
Courtesy of Dylan VanWeelden

low-wage jobs to get him to the next place. He lived in various places and tried many jobs but never found anything he wanted to commit to. These included commercial fishing in Alaska; working at an animal shelter in Lawrence, Kansas; teaching English for a couple of years in Italy; working as a bike courier in Portland; working in kitchens all over the place, East Coast and West; riding his bike cross-country; running out of money in Aspen, Colorado; and having to stop and get a temping job for a couple of weeks to keep going. Joseph further explains, "I was homeless in New York City, also for a few months in Seattle, spent time in New Orleans, wandered for half a year down in Mexico and Central America, and so on. Even when I bought Tim's frame-building equipment, I had no idea I would be building bikes for this long. But I needed something, and it came at just the right time and was just the right thing. Those were hard-living years, and they took their toll."

Luckily for all those people who love riding their Ahearne or Page Street bicycles, Joseph eventually found something he could really commit to. Beyond building bikes, Joseph maintains a keen interest in writing, reading, and travel, with a particular love for Mexico. He says, "It's such a big, beautiful country, and there's so much to explore." During COVID-19 he also picked up a new hobby—"flying a paraglider, which is incredibly fun. I get out and fly whenever I can."

Ahearne Cycle truck. *Courtesy of Joseph Ahearne*

Geometric front basket. *Courtesy of Joseph Ahearne*

Irish coin fork end cap. *Courtesy of Joseph Ahearne*

Classy stainless-steel dropout. *Courtesy of Joseph Ahearne*

Front rack and head badge. *Courtesy of Billy Sinkford*

Tall Man touring bike. *Courtesy of Billy Sinkford*

Page Street "Viajero" mini velo travel bike. *Courtesy of Joseph Ahearne*

"Primary Concern" fat-tire commuter. *Courtesy of Joseph Ahearne*

Ray R. rear rack profile. *Courtesy of Joseph Ahearne*

Ray R. custom rear rack, painted. *Courtesy of Joseph Ahearne*

Ray R. custom rear rack, unpainted. *Courtesy of Joseph Ahearne*

CULT
65PSI MAX

AMAPOLA CYCLES

HENGELO, THE NETHERLANDS

Every spring, the fields of Javier Valiente's birthplace are filled with the special, intense red color of poppies. This was the inspiration for naming his business Amapola—the Spanish name for poppy flowers. He says, "Poppies are strong even though they look delicate. They are always there, year after year." Although Javier moved away from his birthplace to the Netherlands, he still takes inspiration from the strong, continuing qualities of the poppy flower. In essence, machines that the rider can use for a long time, not ruled by the obsolescence of many materials that surround us today. "Bicycles are timeless vehicles created for enjoyment and to feel free. That feeling is the same for a cyclist of one hundred years ago as it is for a cyclist of today. I am very proud to design and create bicycles and be able to transmit these sensations to my clients," he says. Javier describes his workspace as anywhere his basic tools are, so he can design and create: "There is always a space, even a small one, that I can find to create my bikes. I usually say, 'Small spaces, big projects.'" As this point in time, he works in a big space. So, for now it's "big spaces, giant projects." Javier works mostly alone but always has the support and help of his partner for ideas and opinions. This enriches his designs and projects through gaining another point of view.

Javier uses the fillet-brazing welding technique when constructing his bikes. As he explains, "My torch, oxygen, acetylene, and flux bottles can modify the chemical properties of materials to join them together. They give superpowers

Let the child cycle free, including hand-drawn designs on the frame.
Courtesy of Amapola Cycles

A12APOLA

to those who handle it properly. Normally we do not see the result because it is under the paint, but on a naked bike you can see the work done by the frame builder." Javier has always been drawn to technology, mechanics, and engineering and is grateful to combine his hobby and his work. He says, "I have combined various jobs with my love for cars and motorbikes, and in 2018, I decided to introduce myself to the world of bicycle frame building. At that time, the curiosity about how the bicycle works led me to get some training on bicycle design and construction. And that was the beginning of this journey."

The process of designing and building custom, handmade bicycles for each specific customer is very satisfying. In Javier's opinion, "The interaction with a lot of clients with different needs offers something that series-produced bicycles can't. Especially when you see how the person gets the bike he or she imagined." At the very beginning of each bike project, Javier enjoys seeing how customers react to questions about their personal wishes, riding style, or body measurements. As he points out, normally series-production bicycles have standardized measurements, but humans are not standard. It is through the custom bicycle projects that this uniqueness becomes visible as clients start sharing their answers with great enthusiasm. The process from designing the bike on the computer to realizing and assembling it still impresses him because it is full of contrasts. Javier says, "You can design with the most-advanced software programs, and at the same time you work with the materials as the craftsmen did in the old days. The geometries of the frame are governed by physics to create a manageable bicycle, whilst the design and painting offer the freedom to create anything you could imagine." Javier most likes the bottom bracket because it is the core of the bicycle. "It is here where the movement applied by the cyclist begins and is transmitted to the bicycle. It is the link between human and machine."

Javier's design influences and inspiration for each bike build come from the frame-building discipline, design and artistic expression, and his environment. He also takes inspiration from many design eras, styles, and shapes, though each project interprets those influences differently. For example, "Some of the projects that I have made are influenced by the geometries from the track bikes of the early '90s, or the colors of the racing vehicles of the '60s." Nature and colorimetry also serve as inspiration, with Javier stating that "the bicycle is not only the feeling when you ride it, but also what it conveys to you when you see it." Riders and their different projects have also helped shape his style. "All in all, the rider is in the end the strongest influence in a project. Clients know or develop their taste and preferences throughout our various interactions," he says.

Details of the bottom bracket and personalized serial number.
Courtesy of Amapola Cycles

Whenever possible, Javier likes to deliver a bicycle in person. Although he keeps his customers in touch with the building process through photos and updates, he says, "When they receive the bicycle in person, you can see in their eyes the reward of this journey." Javier recalls a memorable moment with a young client when he received his custom MTB (mountain bike). "I went with him for a short ride in the countryside nearby, so he could test the result and we could check the final adjustments. Seeing the enthusiasm and illumination on his face, the first time he used his MTB bike in a downhill, confirmed to me that I'm able to translate the passion and sensations to my clients."

Even in a dynamic world where things are continually evolving, Javier continues to develop his techniques and style and will always remain working in the "amazing world of bicycles." As Javier says, "Bicycles are part of my life. Some marks on my body remind me of that. With bicycles I have laughed and cried, bled, and sweated, but in essence I have enjoyed every spent moment." Javier recognizes that he is fortunate to live in a country where bicycles play a leading role in all aspects of life. "In the Netherlands, bicycles have shaped the way people commute or how cities are built. It influences a lot of the use and enjoyment of bicycles. This has given me the context to better understand how the bicycle interacts with its environment."

When he's not building bikes, Javier's usually out riding them, whether it be surrounded by nature or riding through cities. He also likes things made with passion and soul. "Like a good meal at home, brewing some craft beer in my garage or a well-brewed coffee. Traveling as sustainably as possible is also important. "I like to see that in a society ruled by tight schedules and standard goods, there are still ways to escape and enjoy things in a different way. Being exposed to the elements makes me appreciate being part of the environment in the place where I am."

Taking a break in the forest with cargo bicycle. *Courtesy of Amapola Cycles*

Contemplating the first results and details of a very special gravel bicycle. *Courtesy of Amapola Cycles*

Specially configured gravel bicycle built for fun.
Courtesy of Amapola Cycles

Not another boring commuter bicycle, this encompasses style, design, and functionality. *Courtesy of Amapola Cycles*

Enduro bicycle designed to cope with any obstacle.
Courtesy of Amapola Cycles

Track bicycle built with new old stock materials from the '90s. *Courtesy of Amapola Cycle.*

Amapola is inspired by the delicacy, brightness, and endurance of the poppy flower. *Courtesy of Amapola Cycles*

Letting creativity run free on the paintwork for this road bicycle. *Courtesy of Amapola Cycles*

ALBION

ARGONAUT CYCLES

BEND, OREGON, US

Argonaut bikes are made by a team of passionate, talented, and creative people who believe they are changing the way carbon bikes ride. "Our focus on ride quality has enabled riders to get the most out of every ride. If the ride feels better and is more enjoyable, the chances are you will want to ride longer and more often. We love to ride, and so do the people who ride our bikes. We just want to make everyone's experience better," they say.

Argonaut Cycles was founded in 2007 by Ben Farver. Although their roots are in steel, they saw its limitations and, instead, recognized the potential to really move the bike design needle by using carbon fiber. As they point out, "We quickly realized that if we wanted to add to the conversation of bike design, we were going to have to charge forward with composites, where we are able to do so much more with custom fitting, custom tuning, and performance-centric bikes."

The aim was to redefine the ride quality and performance of carbon bikes by pushing the boundaries of what is possible in the pursuit of perfection. This led them to patent their HPSM (high-pressure silicone molding) manufacturing process. As they explain, "It has enabled us to control the ride quality of our carbon bikes. With HPSM, there are no voids, pinholes, or other structural flaws in any of the parts coming out of our oven." They say their manufacturing process allows them to do not only custom geometry but, more importantly, custom layup patterns: "This enables us to tune the ride quality of every bike we make, based on rider's physiology, weight, power output, preferred terrain, and desired ride quality. The rider is the center of our process."

Argonaut's bright, modern workspace sits in the epicenter of cycling in Bend, Oregon, a stone's throw from miles of single-track, endless gravel roads and inspiring road rides. When not building bikes, they say, "We live to be outdoors. We slide on snow, slide on waves, and love to explore the world."

Argonaut Supernaut GR3 gravel bike.
Courtesy of Argonaut Cycles

Argonaut Custom RM3 road bike. *Courtesy of Argonaut Cycles*

Argonaut Supernaut RM3 road bike. *Courtesy of Argonaut Cycles*

Argonaut Custom RM3 road bike. *Courtesy of Argonaut Cycles*

Argonaut Supernaut GR3 gravel bike. *Courtesy of Argonaut Cycles*

Argonaut Custom GR3 gravel bike. *Courtesy of Argonaut Cycles*

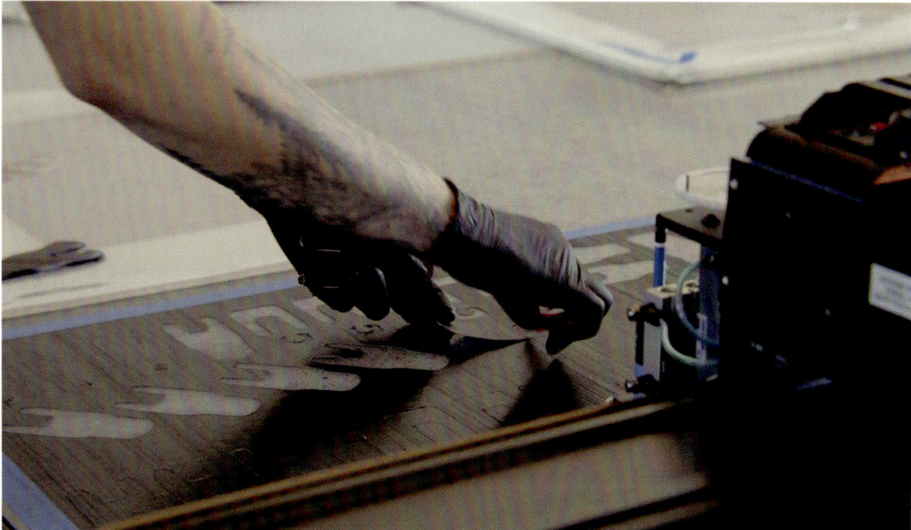

High-pressure silicon molding, layup process.
Courtesy of Argonaut Cycles

Argonaut custom composite layup pattern.
Courtesy of Argonaut Cycles

Argonaut custom GR3 gravel bike.
Courtesy of Argonaut Cycles

ATELIER DES VÉLOS

JUJURIEUX, FRANCE

Like many bicycle builders, Quentin Polizzi rode bikes from a very young age and then gained his first job in a bike shop when age fourteen. His passion for bikes led him to a twenty-five-year immersion into the world of bicycles, during which his enthusiasm has only grown: "While my approach has evolved through learning experiences and skill upgrades, my passion remains unwavering. Today, I believe that the essence of my work lies in crafting intelligent and aesthetically pleasing bikes with innovative components."

Before establishing Atelier des Vélos (ADV), Quentin managed seven Cyclable stores in Paris until 2012. He then began manufacturing bikes independently, creating around forty bikes, mostly for friends. By 2020, he was ready to launch his own business and opened his ADV workshop to customers: "Now, I offer custom bicycle frames in various materials (steel, stainless steel, carbon, and titanium), personalized paints, and 3-D parts for carbon bikes. In my view, ADV represents bike expertise that can cater to diverse preferences, and always with joy."

Quentin typically works alone but occasionally opens his workshop to those interested in frame building: "I mainly teach basic know-how and weld-braze fundamentals to students." He describes his workshop as a modest 40-square-meter room on the first floor containing his tools and equipment, which also features a 6-square-meter space dedicated to paintwork. The most thrilling part of a bike build is when a customer gives him full creative freedom to build their bike. He says, "Having a free hand in the design process, working with steel material, and perfecting the bike with vibrant and unique painting is incredibly satisfying. I invest my mind and energy into creating an outstanding bike!" Likewise, he finds great joy in a customer's excitement when they see their bike for the first time: "I witness the customer's delighted expression when they discover their bike, just like a child unwrapping a Christmas present. Their contagious happiness keeps a smile on my face for days."

If Quentin were to choose a favorite bike frame design feature, for him it is the head badge. In his view, "The head badge is the frame's masterpiece, symbolizing sensitivity, identity, and craftsmanship. But also, I would add that the paint, the first thing that catches the eye, is a very important aesthetical detail." His main design influences come from artists such as Julie Racing Design (France) and Bishop (UK): "Their work inspired me to embark on frame building, a truly stunning craft."

During any free time away from his workshop, Quentin enjoys mountain biking and road cycling, windsurfing, or simply going out for a walk to get some fresh air: "The Ain region, where I live, offers beautiful spots and landscapes, providing the perfect environment for relaxation. Additionally, I'm currently renovating an old house I purchased several months ago. I just can't get enough of building or biking."

Complete bike. One travel bike in steel made for me; the bike of my dream ;). I've painted every part of this bike when it's possible. *Courtesy of Crea Lens Film*

Titanium road bike. The first titanium bike made at the workshop (2024). *Courtesy of Léandre Chéron*

Titanium bike details: integrated seat post with 3-D-printing parts. *Courtesy of Léandre Chéron*

Titanium road bike; detail of the paint of the fork, with rainbow colors. *Courtesy of Léandre Chéron*

Titanium bike details: head badge. *Courtesy of Léandre Chéron*

Personal travel bike detail—cat hidden in the fork. I have three cats at home. I've hidden two of the cats inside the fork. *Courtesy of Léandre Chéron*

Travel bike detail—the other cat on the fenders ;). *Courtesy of Léandre Chéron*

Travel bike detail—head badge inside the front rack. *Courtesy of Léandre Chéron*

Steel MTB from the front, one of my favorite bikes I've made. The paint job is fabulous. *Courtesy of Léandre Chéron*

Details of this MTB. *Courtesy of Léandre Chéron*

BAUM
DURA-ACE

BAUM CYCLES

NORTH SHORE, VICTORIA, AUSTRALIA

With over twenty-five years of experience as a frame builder, Darren Baum has a lot of stories, plenty of insight, and, of course, a large body of work. And in that body of work, there is something that very few frame builders have ever achieved: a steady evolution that has kept pace with, and capitalized on, innovations within the bicycle industry.

Consider the flagship bike that he built for himself in 1996 and kick-started his career as a professional frame builder. It was a silver brazed frame with Columbus EL-OS tubing, hand-polished Henry James stainless-steel lugs, and a steel unicrown fork. A deep-blue gloss finish was the perfect choice to make the shiny lugs pop, and the top tube was labeled with a simple moniker, "Custom," which alluded to the experience gained after spending seven years practicing and refining his craft.

"That bike had a lot of firsts," recalls Baum. "It was the first time that I tried to assemble all my ideas for a tailored road bike, and I was kind of proud of it." It was a stunning bike that quickly won him new customers, but twenty-five years later, it bears little resemblance to his current flagship road bike, the Orbis. In fact, the uninitiated might find it hard to believe that the same person was responsible for both bikes.

Every Orbis, including this Orbis + all-road bike, is made from titanium tubing that is custom-butted to carefully tune the ride quality of the bike to suit each customer. *Courtesy of Spurlo Style Photography*

Like any good custom bike, the Orbis is made to measure, using size-specific tubing, but titanium is now Darren's material of choice, and he depends on TIG (tungsten inert gas) welding to bring the frame to life. An external butting process is used to tune the front triangle according to the needs of the customer, and the rest of the frame is equally bespoke. For example, the head tube and T47 bottom bracket shell are machined in-house according to Darren's specifications, and a series of complex bending and shaping processes are required to create the asymmetrical chainstays.

Of course, Darren did not arrive at the Orbis in a single leap. First, there was the Ristretto, a daring TIG-welded steel frame with a stratospheric price that was unveiled to the public in 2002. Next came the Corretto, which translated all the lessons learned with the Ristretto into titanium for 2007 and ultimately provided the DNA for the Orbis.

A closer look at Baum's brake hose integration strategy for the Orbis, which requires a custom IS52/IS52 head tube that is billet-machined in-house from a solid bar of 6/4 titanium. *Courtesy of Spurlo Style Photography*

A variety of factors were responsible for driving this remarkable evolution, the most important of which is Darren's insatiable curiosity and an innate drive to explore and improve his craftsmanship. This was something present at an early age while growing up in the workshop environment, followed by an apprenticeship in heavy-aircraft maintenance that gave him a fast track into the world of engineering. That was when he discovered a passion for bespoke engineering that would fuel his work as a frame builder for the next two decades. "I loved working in aircraft maintenance, but they gave me a set of rules that I had to work to. I felt like I was doing more-complicated work and working harder at making decisions when I was building a bike."

Any conversation with Darren Baum about frame building inevitably touches on tooling, that interface where the theoretical aspects of engineering are converted into the realities of production. Identifying, modifying, or even creating these tools is an ongoing preoccupation of Baum's, a necessary evil perhaps, but there is a sense that he finds as much satisfaction in finalizing the tooling for a new production process as he does in bringing that part to life. If it is a chore, then the weight of it is likely alleviated by his enthusiasm for new technology and the way it can facilitate his aspirations.

Even though Baum's frame building evolved under its own set of forces, it occurred in the context of an industry undergoing its own evolution. Thus, the quill stem, threaded 1-inch headset, rim brakes, and quick-release axles that were an integral part of Baum's 1996 custom road bike are not just outdated, but completely incompatible with current road bike design. In their place, we have clamp-on stems, oversized threadless headsets, disc brakes, and through-axles, among others, that must be accommodated when building a new frame today.

The interplay between bicycle components and frame design is therefore strong, and manufacturers (big or small) can strengthen their appeal by being quick to adopt a new standard or a revolutionary component design. Baum, however, prefers to bide his time until its longevity has been proven, both in terms of its function and availability. "I want to make a product that will stand the test of time and works so well that you forget about it."

After more than twenty-five years as a frame builder, Baum remains undecided: "I couldn't tell you what my true passion is, riding a bike or actually building it." There was a point early in his career when Darren was more focused on the sport than the craft. Indeed, he might have preferred a career as a road cyclist, except his legs never quite developed the same promise as his hands. Darren never gave up competitive cycling, and to this day he will find the time for a long stint in the saddle, whether or not a race number is pinned to his jersey. Clearly, cycling is an important outlet, but he also depends on it to inform his craft. For example, when he started exploring the nuances of frame geometry, he would make a change to the frame at night, then ride it in his local bunch the next morning. Decades later, Baum's frame designs are still informed by this empirical approach, and all new products are subjected to in-house testing before they can be recommended to his customers.

No discussion of Baum's work is complete without mentioning the finish of his frames, which has evolved at much the same rate as his frame building. He was one of the few titanium frame builders to embrace paint when so many opted for a raw finish, eventually drawing inspiration from automotive racing to elevate and distinguish his bikes. Needless to say, Darren has always considered the finish an important commodity, devoting as much time and resources to its research and development as any other aspect of his craft. The results bear this out, since a Baum frame is arguably more recognizable on the basis of its finish than any of the studious engineering that went into creating it in the first place.

If there is a secret to Baum's success as a frame builder—or at least, his ability to create consistently beautiful bikes—then it might be this: All the effort that is devoted to the design and engineering of the frame and then its eventual finish is always done in the context of the complete bike. "When I get it right, nobody notices it. That's the aim for the frame, the fit, and the whole bike."

Darren Baum has devoted himself to mastering every aspect of frame building, including the science of bike fitting, which he believes is crucial to the performance of the final product. *Courtesy of Spurlo Style Photography*

Every bike bearing the Baum name, including this Orbis, is proudly fabricated by Darren and his small team of specialists in the port city of Geelong in Victoria, Australia. *Courtesy of Spurlo Style Photography*

Baum's workshop is equipped with all the tooling required to fabricate its frames, including this tube notcher, which turns a straight cut into a notch that will sit perfectly flush with the head tube for welding.
Courtesy of Spurlo Style Photography

The intense heat required to weld a frame can lead to distortion, which is why the head tube must be reamed and faced after welding. Baum elects to use a lathe for this process for the best possible result.
Courtesy of Spurlo Style Photography

In addition to all the necessary tooling, Baum's workshop also houses a paint shop for creating the brand's distinctive finishes. A series of masks are used to paint every feature, including the intricate logos.
Courtesy of Spurlo Style Photography

The Celaris is Baum's most recent creation, which shares much of its DNA with the Orbis, but Darren drew inspiration from the classic era of road bikes when deciding on the final look and feel of the bike.
Courtesy of Spurlo Style Photography

A custom 3-D-printed titanium fork insert was created for the Celaris so that the brake housing could be internally routed through a standard stem and headset. *Courtesy of Spurlo Style Photography*

Half-inch seat stays were once a common feature of lugged steel frames—like the ones Darren built during the '90s—and provide a classic touch for the Celaris. *Courtesy of Spurlo Style Photography*

The wall of fame, mainly to save some space.
Courtesy of Chipo Sikumba

BCB (BOUCIF CUSTOM BIKES)

LEUVEN, BELGIUM

According to Driss Boucif, BCB (Boucif Custom Bikes) emerged from a school project. He describes himself as "never an A-grade student." A friend told him about a technical school where you could study moped bicycle and lawnmower mechanics. He admits that most people didn't think it was a good idea to drop out of the classic school system to become a mechanic. But, as he says, "being a seventeen-year-old adolescent, with a 50 cc Kawasaki moped, there was no way I wasn't going to that school!" Already moped obsessed, Driss wanted to learn more about mopeds and how to make them go faster. By undertaking the course, "I went from hating school to absolutely loving it, and from being a bit lost to finding some direction in my life." The course allowed him to also learn about combustion engines, and over time he gained an even-bigger interest in the way that motorcycles handle.

Driss admits that learning about bicycles initially didn't interest him much. His dream was to become a mechanic in a motorcycle-racing team, but an exchange opportunity in France to join an official racing team didn't go through. He says, "For me it was all about motorcycles, but the love and passion for the simple and humble bicycle grew quickly." It was their sense of freedom, speed, and accessibility that appealed. He says, "The genius invention of a single-track vehicle fascinated me. The way it rides instinctively and especially the way it corners; no other type of vehicle can give that magic sensation." As it turned out, his school project required him to make one "special" bike by the end of the year. Instead, he made five bikes with custom frames and handbuilt wheels. The bikes included a city bike with two seats, a racing bike, a mountain bike on big slicks, a cruiser bike with a springer fork, and a special single-speed sidewalk racer. He says, "After that, I kept on making custom bikes for every possible use I could think of."

For Driss, a bike's frame is its soul. He says, "You can change literally anything on a bike, but if you keep the same frame, it's still the same bike. If you keep every part of a bike but change the frame, it won't be the same bike anymore." He began experimenting by altering bike frames and playing with the geometry to get bicycles to handle the way he liked it. But his self-confessed "wild riding style" led to frequent broken forks, bends, and breaks. This taught him an important lesson: "Steel was the ultimate material for me, because when it broke it always came with a warning. First bending, then tearing, and eventually cracking." In his opinion, this was favorably compared to aluminum, which usually snaps without warning.

The classic BCB frame dressed up with state-of-the-art componentry thanks to the SRAM inclusivity scholarship. *Courtesy of Adam Gasson*

In theory, BCB is a one-man operation. But Driss is very rarely alone. His shop is always open for everybody who wants to chill, chat, work on their bike, or just drink beers and listen to music. "It's quite messy and busy, but I really enjoy the atmosphere and being surrounded by so many people during the day." This means that he gets most of his work done during the night, often finishing the bikes he couldn't work on during the day while chilling with his friends. The location of his workshop and the bike culture of Leuven also greatly influence the bikes he builds. His workshop is in "an old high-voltage cabin/chamber next to an indoor skatepark; right in front of one of our city's best street spots." One of its great advantages, he says, is that he has a lot of passing traffic. It's close to the station, and the bike lane located in front of his shop is used by everyone heading to the city: "It's a crazy location and a real hotspot for youngsters. I spend a lot of time just hanging in front of my shop with whoever comes by. There's also a weekly wheelie ride out with a bunch of cool kids!" Leuven is largely a student city where literally everybody rides a bike because that's the way people move around. Driss has also adapted to different bike trends. For example, "When everybody started to ride vintage race bikes, I started to supply sturdy and affordable antipuncture tires so those bikes would be reliable and more fun to ride through the city. And that way I had more time for other stuff than fixing punctured tires all day!"

Driss enjoys every aspect of the processes and milestones of a bike build, particularly when the wheels are fitted in the frame, because you can really see it come together: "Next best is taking it for the first test ride, where you get a taste of the handling and what needs adjusting." Prior to starting any build, there's the excitement of getting to know clients and their lifestyles, and brainstorming to figure out the perfect bike for them. He says, "New ideas will often emerge regarding a nice extra feature." Since Driss likes to reuse bike parts, often retrieved from trashed bikes, it's exciting when he can match a nice part to meet the person's needs. Driss also draws on a number of influences when designing his bikes. According to him, the ultimate design sweet spot of durability and performance of bikes and motorcycles was the late '80s to late '90s. He says, "Stuff from earlier was even more durable but lacked the high performance, and everything from 2000 onward gradually started to lose quality to make room for even-better performances."

Of all his customers, Driss's most treasured is his fiancée. As the story goes, "She first came to my shop to get her bike repaired, then kept coming back with every bike she had." He eventually built her a BCB with a custom frame for Christmas. He says, "With so much passion put into that bike build, I knew she was the one."

A messy workspace gives more room for creativity. *Courtesy of Chipo Sikumba*

(*Opposite top*) Going high tech on this build, cutting hydraulic hoses for the first time. *Courtesy of Chipo Sikumba*

Spot-welding the frame. *Courtesy of Chipo Sikumba*

The tools can be all over, but they aren't always missing!
Courtesy of Chipo Sikumba

BCB head badge, applied only when the bike has earned her wings! *Courtesy of Chipo Sikumba*

One of the kids testing out the latest build. *Courtesy of Chipo Sikumba*

BCBs are built for everyday use on the streets, surviving those occasional crashes. *Courtesy of Chipo Sikumba*

Heavy-duty touring bike. *Courtesy of Chipo Sikumba*

Youngsters living their best life in and around the shop. *Courtesy of Chipo Sikumba*

Bilenky
RECORD

BILENKY CYCLE WORKS

PHILADELPHIA, PENNSYLVANIA, US

Stephen Bilenky has been working on bikes for sixty years. So, in his words, "I think I can safely say that "bikes" is what I do and who I am." As early as ten years old, he was fixing the bikes of neighborhood friends in his parents' garage. These repairs gave him the opportunity to "'research' what made kids' bikes faster," Stephen says. His bike mechanic abilities led him to secure a job at the local Schwinn dealership in Northeast Philadelphia when age twelve. He maintained that position through high school and went on to manage the shop through what he describes as "the bike boom years."

His next move was to open his own shop in 1977, called "The Bike Doctor." Although it was originally a repair-only shop, the many frame repair projects eventually led him to "torch on metal fixes and modifications." This work further inspired him to create user-friendly bike designs out of the previous decade's "ten-speed" bikes. Stephen says, "My first production bike was a lightweight roadster for commuters—my answer to the upcoming surge of MTBs for practical urban transport." He branded them "Sterling." From the beginning, he envisioned a brand that was beyond the one-builder, one-at-a-time workshop to emulate the midsized European bike builders. That is, "Small enough to meet the needs of individual customers but also large enough to have a commercial output of bikes." Stephen decided to focus on a particular range of bikes—"bikes built for women and small-statured riders, long-distance tourists, serious commuters, and couples that ride together on tandem bikes."

Patina-finish artisan track bike. *Courtesy of Brad Quartuccio*

Bilenky bikes have been crafted inside Stephen's 1,500-square-foot, one-story workshop, next to an auto salvage yard, since 1992. He describes his workspace as "decades of collected tools, machines, and projects, resulting in cramped quarters, but I like to refer to it as my 'happy, dirty place.'" The size of his team has fluctuated over the years, but he currently has three part-time assistants, a builder, and a mechanic, plus two serious full-time trainees. As Stephen says, "There is always someone showing up at my door or my inbox unannounced, wanting to work for / learn from me." After thirty-plus years of designing and constructing bikes, Stephen still experiences "enthusiasm rushes." This happens particularly when he is using his favorite technique, fillet brazing, which joins steel tubes by using a torch flame applied to a filler metal: "I love seeing how the individual tubes/fittings lose their individuality and become a unified, flowing structure." He also enjoys solving fabrication and design challenges on the fly as they inevitably occur.

Stephen takes inspiration from a vast array of design influences. He says that anything from "the classic lightweights, especially British builders of the '60s, '70s, and '80s, to flowers, trees, buildings, old tools and machines, and fashion." He also notes that with "the explosion of new builders (and the internet), it makes for a constant supply of previously unfamiliar frame and bike images to digest." The city location of his US East Coast workshop also shapes a lot of his bike builds. They range from the practical everyday and delivery bicycles to the ultimate touring, travel, or randonneuring (long-distance cycling) bike for customers looking to escape the city on weekends.

As one can imagine, Stephen has a lot of memorable customer stories after years of frame building. Two such stories come to mind. He says, "A couple [of] years ago, I was commissioned by the Biden administration to create a custom bike as a gift to a foreign head of state who, like the US president, was an avid cyclist." He is also aware of a YouTube channel video where "someone posted about how their fifteen-year-old custom Bilenky cargo bike changed his life. What started for him as a way to promote and develop a zero-emissions photography business grew into a full-time career as a bicycle lifestyle influencer."

Though Stephen has been building bikes for decades, he almost pursued a different career path: "I attended college for Agricultural science, so I tried to get into farming when I first graduated. I also did research on sustainable farming practices and authored a funded National Science Foundation grant "Community Design for Optimal Energy and Resource Utilization". So, there was a small glimmer of pursuing an academic career. When that didn't pan out, I devoted myself to music while simultaneously running my bike repair shop." Luckily for all the Bilenky owners out there, he dedicated his creative talents to building bikes.

Cat marketing team always on task at BCW. *Courtesy of Bilenky Cycle Works*

Stephen hand-slotting a seat tube. *Courtesy of Daniel Maloney*

Bilenky Cycle Works has won many awards at national shows for best bike types and construction quality. In 2014, Stephen was selected for a Balvenie Master Craftsman Award. According to the American Craft Council website, "The Balvenie was presented in recognition and support of contributions to the maintenance and revival of traditional or rare crafts in America." On a less-serious note, Stephen says, "I'm throwing down the gauntlet to anyone who can find earlier documentation than mine of my signature 'bike cap and beard' that has become the iconic 'look' of a new generation of cyclists and frame builders." As seen in the Rare Craft Fellowship Awards photo section![11] He was also featured in an episode of the Craftsman's Legacy series, which he says, "continues to be aired periodically on PBS Network television."

When he's not building bikes or administering and maintaining his bike business, he says he's teaching frame building and reconnecting to his music. "I teach a course several times a year at the Metal Guru frame-building school and usually have an in-shop intern." He's also getting back into songwriting, with some of his compositions being considered for film and TV placements.

Titanium tandem elegance. *Courtesy of Bilenky Cycle Works*

Keystone Crusher Lite with painter's choice finish.
Courtesy of Bilenky Cycle Works

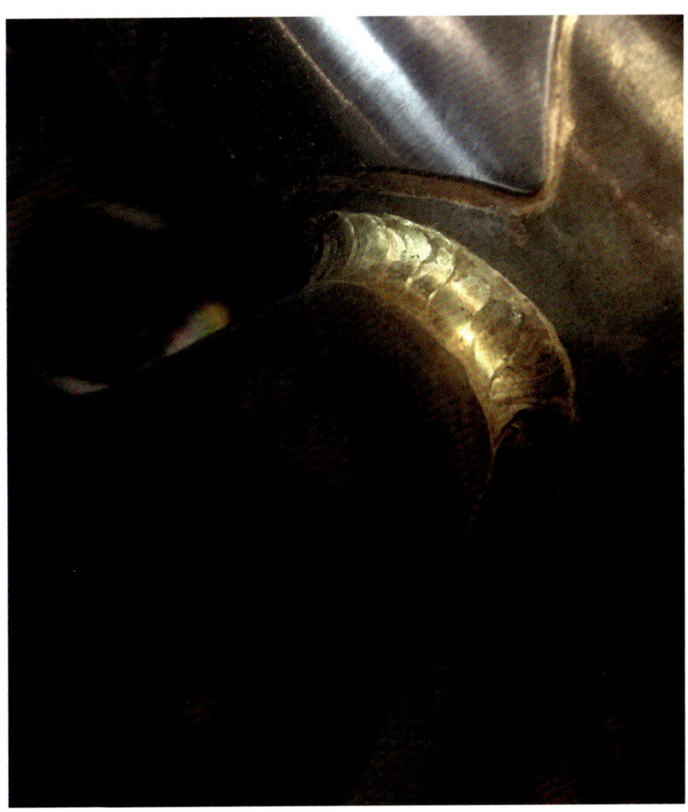

Flo-braze responding to the Coriolis force. *Courtesy of Bilenky Cycle Works*

Artisan Travel Midlands. *Courtesy of Nick McCormick*

Artisan hedgehog. *Courtesy of Philadelphia Magazine*

Graduation Day at Metal Guru Fillet brazed-frame-building class.
Courtesy of Conor Urian

Vintage British lugs on a modern BCW build.
Courtesy of Bilenky Cycle Works

PRAXIS
M30

CALFEE DESIGN

LA SELVA BEACH, CALIFORNIA, US

Craig Calfee lives in a beautiful area immersed in natural beauty. Sandwiched between the redwood forests and the Pacific Ocean, he doesn't have to look far to find inspiration for the bikes he and his team build. Craig has a long history of manufacturing bikes, particularly carbon, beginning with his Tetra, built in 1987. According to Craig, this was at a time when "carbon was considered a passing fad." Since 1987, the Tetra has been manufactured continuously, using the same "signature gussets at tube junctions." In fact, Craig claims that "the Tetra has been in production longer than any other carbon bike.[12] The Tetra's other claim to fame was that Greg LeMond, former American road-racing cyclist, rode the Tetra, as defending champion, at the 1991 Tour de France.[13]

Craig Calfee is also known for his bamboo bikes. He first started building with bamboo in 1995, after realizing how strong it was as a building material. What started out as a gimmick build for a trade show in 1995, Calfee bamboo bikes went into production and remain a staple feature of the Calfee brand. Craig's interest in bamboo bikes also has extended to helping people in Africa build their own bamboo bikes, where it grows in abundance: "Now there are bamboo bikes being made in Ghana, Uganda, Zambia, Liberia, and the D.R. Congo."[14]

Detail shot of the Cephal bottom bracket area.
Courtesy of Drew Rogers

For Craig, "Bikes are the most elegant transport solution" because they enhance our ability to move from place to place. The bicycle is also constantly improving and evolving and so remains a "fun focus of creativity and inventiveness," he says. Calfee bikes are designed and created in a building at the Monterey Bay Academy, which sits on the bluff overlooking the Pacific Ocean. One of the many advantages of the location is the year-round riding weather, which allows full test rides anytime. California is full of people who are active on all kinds of bikes, and that keeps the fifteen staff, including Craig, busy building new bikes, undertaking carbon frame repairs, working on various carbon fiber parts, and retrofitting older bikes into e-bikes. According to Craig, the favorite workshop tool is the Sizer Cycle, which is a stationary fitting bike that is adjustable while the rider is pedaling. As he points out, "It allows a person to quickly find the sweet spot of a particular dimension on the bike. Getting the fit correct is so very important. It all starts with a proper fitting." Craig looks to nature for design solutions, where form following function is apparent. He says, "With millions of years of evolution, the design of most 'parts' found in nature is perfect for the intended task. This is usually easy to translate into composites where fiber orientation aligns with the flow of the stresses."

Craig Calfee holding his latest creation: an aero-tubed racing tandem. *Courtesy of Drew Rogers*

Craig and his team find that the exciting part of a bike build comes when a particular customer, who has usually owned nice bikes, takes delivery of their dream bike. Craig says, "Their custom-built bike is usually their 'last' bike that represents the culmination of their passion for cycling. It's a privilege to build this level of bicycle for such discerning people." When it comes to satisfied customers, Craig recalls a particularly endearing encounter with the comedian/actor Robin Williams:

> I was at the Escape from Alcatraz race expo, showing our bikes, and Robin Williams and a small entourage walk up to our booth and ask for me. I came forward and introduced myself, not recognizing him just yet. He drops to his hands and knees like I was a king, and he starts into a dramatic monologue of how wonderful it is to meet the "master frame builder" and what an honor it is to ride one of my creations, etc. It was uproariously funny, and a small crowd gathered for the free entertainment. Then he stood up and became serious for a minute and told me, "I have twenty bikes in my garage that I can ride any time, but my favorite one is the Tetra Custom you built for me." Then I showed him the bamboo bike on display. Off he went, spooling out every joke you can imagine about bamboo bikes, including my favorite, which he breathlessly ended with "And you have to ride faster than a hungry panda!"

Craig Calfee's creative skills have always been in demand. Prior to building bikes, he describes his work life as high-end woodworking for a variety of rock stars in the San Francisco music scene. "I was building out their dreams for interior cabinets and shelves. I had to turn down some interesting work when I started building Greg LeMond's team racing bikes." When he's not building bikes, Craig says you can find him "riding the tandem with his wife, going to his kids' basketball games, participating at Burning Man, sailing friends' boats, and teaching bamboo bike building in developing countries."

"Patsquatch" testing out the Cephal in Utah. *Courtesy of Drew Rogers*

The original BarStem. Custom-length stem and handlebar combination wrapped together as a unified structure. *Courtesy of Drew Rogers*

Craig Calfee adjusting the brakes on a Bamboo Tandem. *Courtesy of Drew Rogers*

Opposite: The form-follows-function aesthetic with a splashy purple metallic paint finish. *Courtesy of Drew Rogers*

A Calfee Bamboo Tandem featuring square bamboo and an electric-assist carbon fiber Tetra Tandem with couplers for travel. *Courtesy of Drew Rogers*

Marbleized teal paintwork on a Calfee carbon fiber Dragonfly Tandem. *Courtesy of Drew Rogers*

Two custom bikes showing the range of sizes that can be made at Calfee Design. *Courtesy of Drew Rogers*

The Calfee Big Adventure, on the bluff, dreaming of flying. *Courtesy of Drew Rogers*

Opposite: "Patsquatch" carving a turn just below the treeline. *Courtesy of Drew Rogers*

Ernest Csuka, after sixty years of craftmanship, working on one of his last frames (2006). *Courtesy of Cycles Alex Singer*

CYCLES ALEX SINGER

LEVALLOIS-PERRET, PARIS, FRANCE

Olivier Csuka says he was "born" in the Cycles Alex Singer workshop, which has operated from the same location for eighty-five years. After observing and helping Ernest Csuka, his father, who worked there from 1944 until 2009, Olivier eventually "took over the torch." With Olivier's fifty years of riding and thirty-five years of competition know-how, his philosophy toward bikes is simple: "Don't speak about bikes; ride them! And preferably ride the finest bikes, because they give pleasure to riders all over the world."

The story of Cycles Alex Singer began in Hungary, where Alex Singer was a young bike racer. After World War I, Alex came to France to complete in the Montmartre Sportif as a teammate for Henri Pélissier, winner of the 1923 Tour de France.[15] At that time, the movement of "cyclotourism" (touring and sightseeing on bikes) in France was starting, but Alex observed that none of the bikes were built specifically for this activity. "Alex quickly understood he could make a better cyclotourist bicycle," Olivier says. In response, he created his own brand in November 1938, at first specializing in tandems aimed at people on paid vacation leave. In time, Alex's nephews, Ernest and Roland Csuka, joined him in the workshop. Olivier believes that the key to the customized, bespoke bicycles they produce is that Alex, Ernest, and Roland all were great riders. They always designed and constructed their bikes with the rider in mind.

Olivier Csuka seemed destined to build bikes in the Cycles Alex Singer shop. When asked by the schoolmaster or mistress what he wanted to be, his answer was always "WORLD CHAMPION!" "Of what?," they would ask. "Cycling, of course." As Olivier explains, there were no real forks in the road as to what he ended up doing, just steps in the story. Some of those steps were "learning to ride without hands"(1968), short rides with our mother (1970), discovering club rides (1972), my first pass in the mountains (1974), my first race (1980), a crash in a race, which prevented me from reaching my potential (1985), and the early death of my mother (1986), which led to starting to help my father more with the work. There was also the beginning of my career in an insurance company (thirty years!), then my best years of riding, from 1986 until 2009, with a few victories." He also discovered the pleasure of rides with his wife and children, Sunday and holiday rides, as well as competing in brevets.

Polymiltipliée Chanteloup 1947: Alex Singer (*left*) and Ernest Csuka (*right*) present Pilotes's bikes. *Courtesy of Cycles Alex Singer*

"After the death of my father (2009), I decided to continue the brand, at first working part time, and since 2017 as my full-time occupation."

Olivier's design influences and inspiration emanate from what he refers to as "the golden age of French handmade bicycles," as well as a registered archive of '70s racing bikes. Memories of the many places, landscapes, brevets, and races also provide him with plenty of inspiration. As for a design theory, Olivier likes to quote the French poet, satirist, and critic Nicolas Boileau: "Slowly make haste, and without losing courage / Twenty times redo your work / Polish and repolish endlessly." And sometimes add, "But often take away."

Olivier never really works alone in the iconic Cycles Alex Singer shop. His son Walter, fourth generation, now works with him, as well as a whole community of people and teammates who come to visit regularly. Naturally, the exciting part begins when a customer enters the shop wanting a new bike. The usual questions follow: Why? How? When? Where? With whom? Then they search for the best solutions. Olivier says, "Inspiration is just to free your mind to be quiet while working. But for the work, only the knowledge." Olivier loves working with his hands, so when asked to nominate his favorite tool, his choice is a good file. As for his favorite bike part, he says, "My stem, handlebar, tape, and front wheel; in fact, what I have always under my eyes while riding. But for efficiency, nothing can go past an excellent frame and pair of wheels." At the end of a bike build, there's the satisfaction of seeing the well-finished frame, which Olivier describes as "like hearing the perfect sound from a bell." It's not until the bike has been delivered to the customer and you hear their feedback after the first ride that you know you have hit the right note.

Olivier retells an inspirational customer story about a tall guy who came into the shop wanting to restart physical exercise. Olivier says, "He was only fifty-eight years old, overweight, and tired from years of physical work. His first thought was to start out riding a bike but never in the rain. Later, I proposed to him that he try riding with our group, but he took a whole year to accept my offer. On the first ride, we waited, pulled, and pushed him, but he returned the next week, then weeks turned into months. Now, he is seventy-four, very fit, owns four bicycles, and was able to finish one of the hardest "Etape du Tour" in Val Thorens, Paris–Roubaix, and many brevets (long-distance rides)."

Olivier during a "Classique" (1991). *Courtesy of Cycles Alex Singer*

When he's not building or riding bikes, Olivier takes time to holiday with family, walk in the mountains, ski, cook, and share a nice wine and meal with friends or Catherine, his wife.

Olivier Csuka at work on a frame (2019). *Courtesy of Christian Bille*

When customers share their passion in the workshop (2021). *Courtesy of Christian Bille*

Team Deloitte Compétition, for Jean Csuka (2017). *Courtesy of Walter Csuka*

The nicest Velotaf, waiting for her master in Paris. *Courtesy of Christian Bille*

Back from chrome. When you are sure you made the best work.
Courtesy of Walter Csuka

Olivier Csuka (2008), Paris–Roubaix, the best test for the bikes and to enjoy how they are faster than others. *Courtesy of Cycles Alex Singer*

After riding many kilometers, the historic monument Mont-Saint-Michel. *Courtesy of Gabriel Refait*

Col de la Madeleine, Mont Blanc, Olivier Csuka (2023). First pass was forty-nine years ago.
Courtesy of Cycles Alex Singer

Paris–Brest–Paris 2023, presentation of the machine.
Courtesy of Ernest Benoit-Ourion for Cyclopast

CYCLES GRAND BOIS

KYOTO, JAPAN

Cycles Grand Bois began in 1987, when Ikuo Tsuchiya opened a bicycle shop after leaving his job at the JNR (Japan National Railways) when it was privatized. As Ikuo points out, "If this privatization had not happened, I would have continued as a railwayman and enjoyed bicycles as a hobby."

The Grand Bois brand name is derived from the name of a mountain pass on the outskirts of Saint-Étienne in south-central France. Ikuo Tsuchiya says, "At the Col de Grand Bois, there is a monument honoring Paul de Vivie (Velocio), who is said to be the father of the French bicycle industry."

It is not surprising, then, that Ikuo draws on some of the French traditional bike builders. In his opinion, "Great bicycle builders like Rene Herse and Alex Singer, who were both at the forefront of the development of touring bikes in France in the 1950s, provide inspiration for his bicycle designs." "Building new bikes with those bikes by my side gives me great inspiration," Ikuo says. He also has a collection of many illustrations left by Mr. Daniel Rebour, editor of *Le Cycle*, from which to draw inspiration.

From 1996 to 2009, Ikuo developed a close working relationship with Mr. Ernest Csuka of Cycles Alex Singer. During this time, he visited Paris with orders from Japan because he wanted to bring as many randonneurs, made by Ernest, to Japan as possible. "I sincerely respected him and learned a lot about bicycle building through our conversations. It was also great when I rode with him all the way to Versailles at Rally Singer in 2007."

Being a fan of bike touring, Ikuo is also inspired by his own touring experiences. He says, "I prefer the speed of a bicycle. The walking speed is too slow to move forward, and the car is too fast to see things on the side of the road. I like cycling, where I can encounter various things and move forward little by little."

The Grand Bois team, comprising three people, manufactures everything from frames to finished bikes. As Ikuo explains, "The Kyoto workshop is a dustproof space where things are assembled, and frames are finished." He also has a home and atelier in the countryside 50 kilometers north of Kyoto, where his frames are manufactured.

Kyoto's natural surroundings and rhythms influence each of his bike builds. As Ikuo points out, "Time moves slowly there, and we can easily get into nature. It is always possible to build a bicycle in a natural and carefully considered manner." There is much satisfaction and excitement when "the bike turns out to be exactly what I expected."

When not building bikes, Ikuo enjoys growing tomatoes, radishes, and red beans in his small, cultivated field in front of his house.

Grandbois randonneur with steel fork and stainless-steel rack.
Courtesy of CYCLESGRANDBOIS

Opposite: Grandbois randonneur with stainless-steel frame. *Courtesy of CYCLESGRANDBOIS*

Grandbois special large hub for cassette sprocket. *Courtesy of CYCLESGRANDBOIS*

A green brass head badge will be attached to this Grandbois special bike. *Courtesy of CYCLESGRANDBOIS*

2019 Paris–Brest–Paris (2019 Concours de machines entry bike, third prize). *Courtesy of CYCLESGRANDBOIS*

2019 Paris–Brest–Paris (2019 Concours de machines entry bike). Around the front, it has complicated electrical wiring and a light switch on the top of the stem. *Courtesy of CYCLESGRANDBOIS*

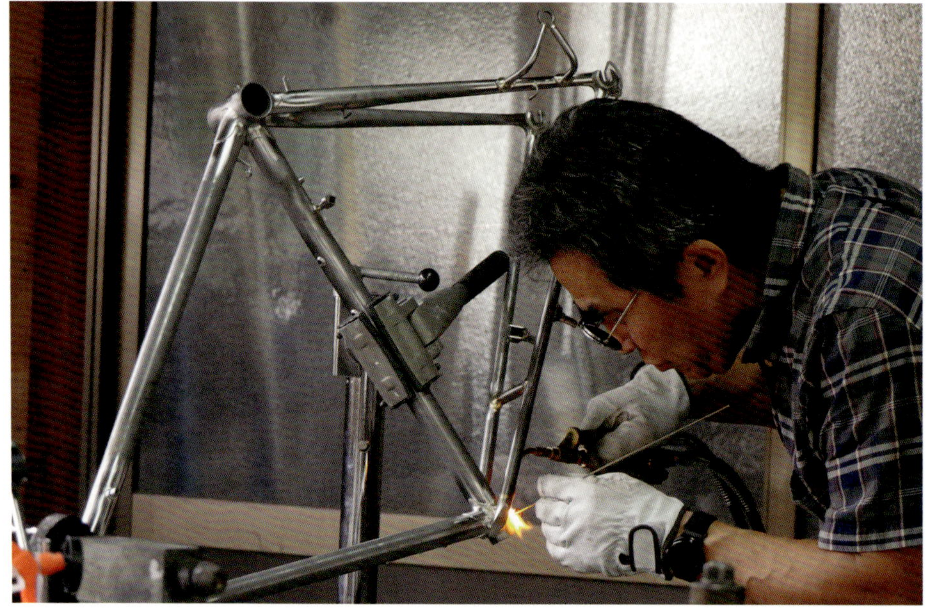

Ikuo making a frame. *Courtesy of CYCLESGRANDBOIS*

Rest at the control point of Paris–Brest–Paris. *Courtesy of CYCLESGRANDBOIS*

Paris–Brest–Paris goal. *Courtesy of CYCLESGRANDBOIS.*

Grandbois touring scenery, Hokkaido Kushiro Wilderness. *Courtesy of CYCLESGRANDBOIS*

DARIO PEGORETTI

VERONA, ITALY

The history and story of Dario Pegoretti, retold here by the Pegoretti team, are a testament to Dario the man and bicycle builder, who, sadly, passed away in 2018: "Our founder, Dario Pegoretti, was racing in a junior team when he married the daughter of Luigino Milani, a well-known frame builder. Dario took an opportunity to become Milani's apprentice. He could never have predicted his legendary status in the bicycle world."

After many years inside the workshop of Luigino Milani, Dario established his own workshop in 1990. He was the man behind the scenes building bikes for champions such as Pantani, Indurain, and Cipollini. The team at Pegoretti particularly makes mention of how Dario created artistic frames called "Ciavete." His creations, inspired by Rothko's paintings, Basquiat's graffiti, and Jackson Pollock's abstract expressionism, have earned a place in design museums and have become collectors' items.

Before his passing, Dario had a dream to see his brand continue and grow in the years to come. His team, comprising Pietro, Andrea, Leonardo, Niccolò, and Cristina, is working to make *his* dream a reality: "If everything starts with the dream of one man, it takes a team to transform it into reality. This is our goal when we come into the "Officina" (workshop) in the morning." Officina Dario Pegoretti continues to be inspired by Dario's unique life vision: "The workshop remains a place for those looking for unique products,

Ciavete paint. *Courtesy of Officina Dario Pegoretti*

Image of our workshop office and showroom.
Courtesy of Officina Dario Pegoretti

built with precision, [high] quality, and timeless style." The team likes to compare their workspace to the "Bottega" of artisans in the Italian Renaissance: "A place where people meet, exchange ideas, come to listen to music, have lunch together, celebrate their birthday, or simply take photos or paint a canvas to hang in the few empty spaces on the walls. It is a place that feels like home with friends and many beautiful pieces collected over the years."

The team's design influences and inspiration are drawn from a range of creative mediums: "Nature, artists, music, and all the people that come to visit and tell us their stories and show us the places where they live or have traveled to." Every new bike build also has its favorite moments. Particularly, performing the TIG welding technique and creating the "Ciavete" paint jobs. Sometimes customers want to have their entire life story represented on the frame: "We smile and say, sorry, it is only eight steel tubes . . . no space for your entire life to ride on." But when the job is complete, "it's always an exciting moment to witness the happiness and emotion of our Pegoretti customer when they pick up their frame or bicycle."

The team's testament to Dario Pegoretti is eloquently summed up with these words: "Even though each member came from different roads and experiences, they all happened to get to the same green traffic light—Officina Dario Pegoretti. But then the traffic light suddenly turned red with Dario's passing. . . . We stood frozen for a few moments and all waited for the green to restart with the same passion and belief of our founder. We all have the same goal—make him proud to work on frames that bear his name. Building frames with the name Dario Pegoretti *is* like having our friend and tutor still with us."

Complete build of Pegoretti bicycle in Ciavete paint. *Courtesy of Officina Dario Pegoretti*

The current Officina Team. *Courtesy of Aaron Guy Leroux (rights by Officina Dario Pegoretti)*

Ciavete paint. *Courtesy of Officina Dario Pegoretti*

Painting a Ciavete frame. *Courtesy of Officina Dario Pegoretti*

Love #3 aluminum-frame complete build.
Courtesy of Officina Dario Pegoretti

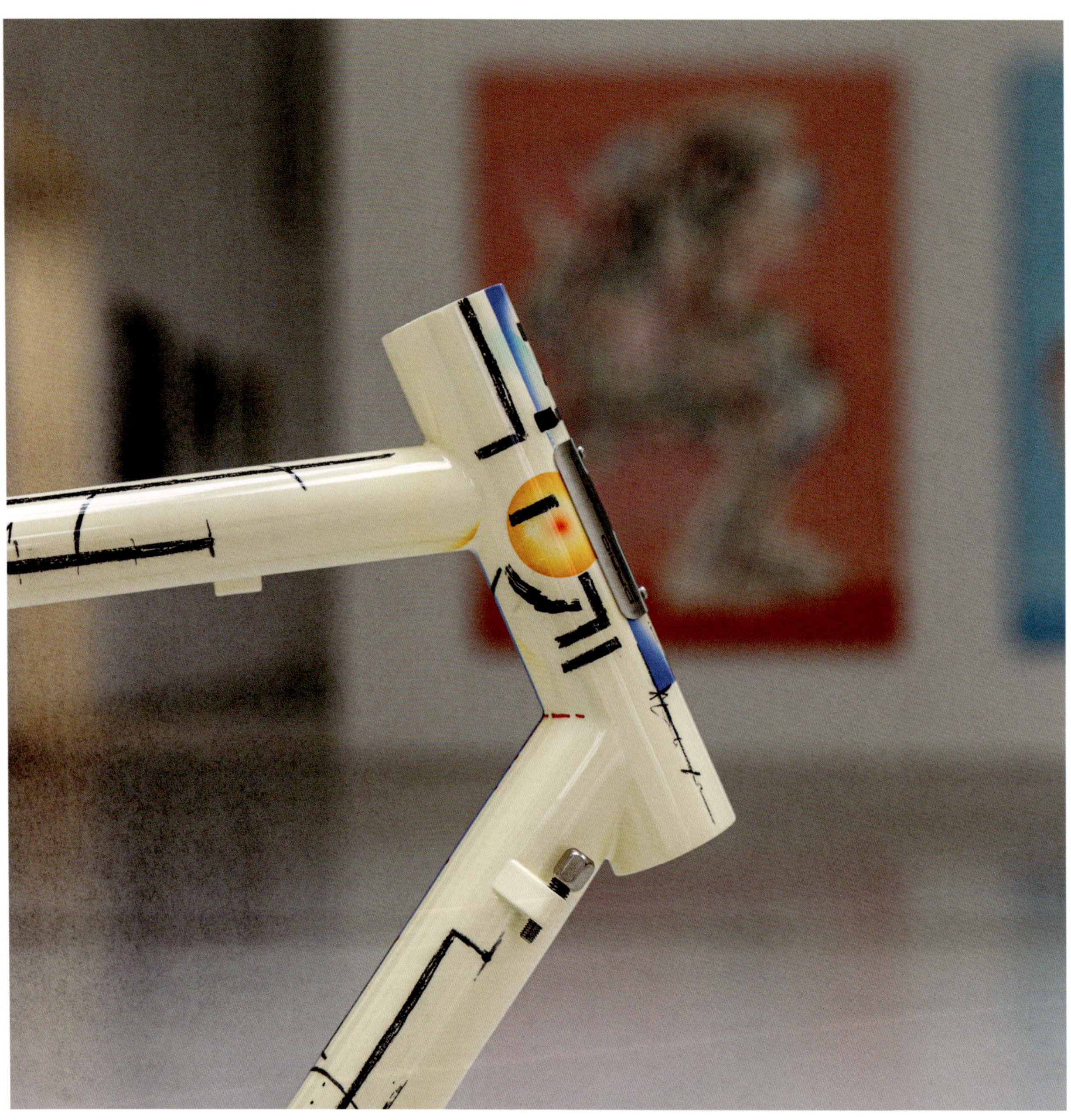

Frame Marcelo model in Ciavete paint.
Courtesy of Officina Dario Pegoretti

Pietro at work to finish the frame. *Courtesy of Aaron Guy Leroux (right of Officina Dario Pegoretti)*

Mesonperso rainbow graphic on Pegoretti frame. *Courtesy of Officina Dario Pegoretti*

STRADA FANGO
ELLIS
THOMSON
FURIOUS FRED
SCHWALBE
XTR

ELLIS CYCLES

FRANKLIN, WISCONSIN, US

David Wages has been working in the bike industry since the late '80s. His passion for bikes began when, as a little kid, he rode his coaster brake Schwinn around his suburban neighborhood: "When my family moved to a rural part of upstate New York, I upgraded to a Raleigh ten speed, and I've never really looked back!"

After gaining his first job assembling kids' bikes in a bike shop, he worked at a couple of more shops before landing a job at Serotta Cycles, working in their final quality control / shipping department in 1994: "I spent a few years doing this job, but about 1997, one of the brazers at Serotta stayed after work and showed me how the torches worked and how to melt brass and braze a fillet." This technique, called fillet brazing, joins steel tubes by using a torch flame applied to a filler metal such as brass. From there, David was hooked. He spent countless hours after work practicing, getting advice, and learning the craft. Not long after, he transferred into Serotta's brazing department. First, he learned how to finish fully brazed frames, then moved on to braze-ons, dropouts, lug prep, and all the other small tasks that add up to a complete brazed frame. After working his way up to head of the brazing department, in 2000 he decided on a life change and packed up and moved west to Wisconsin to work for Waterford Precision Cycles: "Over eight years at Waterford, I built thousands of bikes, developed a custom-carved lug program, and showed several groundbreaking bikes at the North American Handmade Bike Show (NAHBS). In 2008, I felt like the only option left to fully

My very first Strada Fango from 2013, with 29 × 2.0 in. tires and a mix of Dura Ace and XTR parts. *Courtesy of Peter DiAntoni*

express my designs was to strike out on my own, and that's when Ellis Cycles was born." The global recession made the first year tough, but David hung in there and managed to take home an award for Best Lugged Frame at NAHBS in 2009. He says, "In subsequent years, I also won Best in Show (2010), Best Road Frame (2011), Best Steel Construction (2012), and finally Best Fillet Brazed Frame (2014). Over the last fifteen-plus years, I've built hundreds of Ellis frames and sent them all over the world."

After years of working for larger bike manufacturers, David wanted Ellis Cycles to be a one-man shop. By his own admission, his shop is low key, comprising an alignment plate, a large workbench with frame fixture attached, and a fork fixture that can be clamped in a workstand: "Most all of my work is done with dynafiles, a die grinder, hand files, and a disc and belt sander. I do have a drill press, but it is set up to drill seat lugs and fork crowns." As David points out, the ability to individually shape lugs adds a distinctive touch to each one of his bikes. "The uniqueness is something I never get tired of. I'm also excited by where that bike will take me or my clients. I've had some great adventures by bike, and I'm always energized by pictures and letters from rides showing me where their Ellises have taken them."

Though David works mainly with modern components, he has a soft spot for Campagnolo Delta brakes, which were introduced in the mid-'80s when he started to seriously get into cycling and racing. As he recalls, "I spent hours poring through bike magazines to see the coolest new bikes and parts, and I can still remember a picture of a Delta brake in a velvet-lined box from one of the bike shows. They just looked like one of the coolest things I'd ever seen!" Years later, he built a frame for himself with a Campy Record group from about 1990 with Delta brakes, but he never actually rode the frame with those parts on it. After showing the bike at the 2010 NAHBS, he says, "I carefully took all the parts off and returned them to their boxes so they wouldn't have any scratches or damage!"

David says he draws design inspiration from the Italian steel bikes of the '70s and '80s: "Chromed lugs, forks, and

An Ellis Strada Inox with polished stainless-steel main tubes and lugs. *Courtesy of Chris Harris*

James Lalonde winning the 2008 Singlespeed Cyclocross National Championship on his Ellis. *Courtesy of David Wages*

My original shop cat, Alley, inspecting some bilaminate fillets on an early Ellis mountain bike frame. *Courtesy of David Wages*

rear triangles are some of my favorite things. Accordingly, he offers a model called the Modern Classic that incorporates a number of these aesthetic elements, but with modern stainless-steel tubing and lugs polished to a mirror shine. He says, "Ideally, I hope that folks will appreciate the classic aesthetic combined with the modern high-strength steel tubing and modern parts. I can build a very lightweight high-performance steel frame that still harkens back to those steel frames that I coveted in my youth!"

David describes his southeastern Wisconsin environs as a network of rural roads built in the early to mid-twentieth century to help dairy farmers get their milk to market: "Many of these roads, designated as "rustic roads" by the state, make an amazing network for cycling. They are generally very low traffic, allow us to transverse large parts of the state safely, and often across gorgeous landscapes." Gravel bike culture is also alive and well in the region, with some of the oldest rails to trails in the US, which are almost always crushed limestone. Fat biking is also popular because most winters have a fair bit of snow.

Embarking on biking adventures is a significant part of the Ellis Cycles story. In 2018, David's wife quit her job, and he took a couple of months off for them to ride the Sierra Cascades route from Mexico to Canada. He recalls:

> We had done some shorter tours around Wisconsin, but this was a significant bump-up in miles and time on the road. We also don't have mountains in Wisconsin, so those first couple of weeks in Southern California were tough. We rode into Yosemite National Park on Memorial Day weekend, which was not our plan, but because the route was so tough, it took us longer than we anticipated to get to Yosemite. We were worried about the traffic, finding a campsite, the weather, the tunnels, etc. On the second day, we rode up from Wawona and over the large climb, where we descended into the park from the south entrance. When we exited the tunnel and got our first view of the valley, with El Capitan and Halfdome in the distance, it was a life-changing moment. I got goose bumps descending the rest of the way into the valley on our bikes. We still both have so many fond memories of that trip and the amazing sights we witnessed.

Working on bikes was always going to be David's thing. He did study ceramic engineering at university for two semesters but decided that this was never going to be the path for him. So, when he's not building bikes, he says, "I'm an amateur woodworker (the tools share my frame-building space), a cook, and a gardener."

Our 2018 Sierra Cascades tour, looking north toward Mt. Lassen as we ride along Lake Almanor. *Courtesy of Deborah Wages*

My wife Deborah's Modern Classic. *Courtesy of David Wages.*

ELLIS
GRX

Detail of the head lug on the frame above.
Courtesy of Drew Triplett

A classic-looking Strada Fango gravel bike with 38 mm tires and twelve-speed Dura Ace.
Courtesy of David Wages

The "Best Lugged Frame" from the 2009 NAHBS show in Indianapolis, Indiana. *Courtesy of Drew Triplett*

Detail of my sleeved stainless-steel seat stays, which allow for a graceful transition from paint to polished stainless. *Courtesy of Drew Triplett*

gramm
FERN

FERN BICYCLES

BERLIN, GERMANY

Florian Haeussler says, "The bicycle is, by far, the best-ever vehicle created to explore this wonderful world!" The history of Fern Bicycles began in 2006, when Florian headed off on his first big bike journey from Budapest to Istanbul on what he describes as "my shitty old MTB bike." He says, "While cycling through the amazing Balkans, the idea grew that there could be much-better touring bikes." He then vowed to become a frame builder one day.

Florian used to work as a CAD/industrial designer in the automotive industry, designing show cars and prototypes, so he considered his skills as transferable. His wish came to fruition in 2011, when an opportunity to take over a frame-building workshop presented itself. So, he decided to take a chance, bought all the tools, and started learning how to make frames. By the summer of 2012, he took himself and his first self-made Fern prototype bike on a cycling trip around the Black Sea. Florian says, "After 3,500 kilometers, I successfully reached Istanbul again, and the dream of my own frame-building company finally became a reality. Luckily, I discovered cycling and frame building, and eventually I switched from four to two wheels. Still a good choice, I think!"

Starting the long process of a new bike build with a blank piece of paper is always exciting: "From the very first ideas and sketch drawings, then the actual frame building, to designing the paint concept and matching bags, until finally the actual real bike stands in front of us. The best

Nils is having fun! *Courtesy of Stefan Haehnel*

moment is to see the happy, smiling customers when coming back from their first test ride!" It is always amazing to receive postcards or emails of customers happily exploring the world on my bikes. Fern means "far away," and that's why I make bikes!"

From a general design perspective, Florian says he's a "mega fan of Dieter Rams, the product designer who created so many iconic designs for Braun home audio systems. It is the simple clean lines, offering perfect usability that delivers 'form follows function at its best!'" In terms of bicycle design influences, Florian draws on several French bicycle makers from the beginning of last century. Some of these include Rene Herse, Alex Singer, Jo Routens, Narcisse, Reyhand, and Louis Pitard. Florian also acknowledges that the German bike culture and the Berlin frame-builder community is a source of fresh ideas and influences for his own creations. The frame builders have regular meetings, share ideas, and help each other all the time.

Every Fern bike is a product of joined forces and creativity: the frame builder, the bag maker, and the painter. In 2013, Florian's girlfriend, Kristin, started her own company, Gramm Tourpacking, and joined forces with Fern. Her company specializes in handmade bespoke bike-packing and touring-bike bags. As Florian points out, "I do the frame building, Kristin designs and sews the bags, and Robert, our painter, creates the perfectly matching paint jobs." Proximity also plays its part in the production of Fern bikes. Kirstin's and Florian's workshops are in the same building, right next to each other, and Robert's paint shop is just around the corner.

When he's not building and collaborating on bikes, Florian does a bit of cycling and bike touring, loves being outside in nature, and restores historical motorcycles.

A Fern in the wilderness. *Courtesy of Stefan Haehnel*

Fern Chacco. *Courtesy of Stefan Haehnel*

Alignment check. *Courtesy of Stefan Haehnel*

Flo. *Courtesy of Stefan Haehnel*

Rack brazing. *Courtesy of Stefan Haehnel.*

Internal cable routing. *Courtesy of Stefan Haehnel*

Kristin in her workshop. *Courtesy of Stefan Haehnel*

Ingredients for a pannier bag. *Courtesy of Stefan Haehnel*

Robert in his paint workshop. *Courtesy of Stefan Haehnel*

hope
hope

FINNBAR TROUT CYCLES

COLOGNE, NORTH RHINE–WESTPHALIA, GERMANY

The name Finnbar Trout combines two things: a tribute to a beloved dog and a childhood nickname. James Buckley explains, "I'm a typical Pisces, both introvert and extrovert! I wanted a brand that kept me out of the spotlight but had a cheeky humor. Finn was my first dog that was truly mine, a wild hunting terrier with boundless energy. Trout was a nickname I had as a kid, so Finnbar Trout Cycles was born! The brand is a mix of the heritage of steel frame building as I learned it in England with several master builders, and the future, as steel and frame-building materials and techniques have evolved. All mixed together with some Yorkshire pragmatism!"

James's connection to bicycles began with his obsession with anything on wheels—bicycles, motorbikes, and cars. His first set of accessible wheels was his bike, which gave him a sense of freely moving around the small village where he lived: "I then I joined a cycling club, and the horizons expanded. I quickly began racing on road and track, and so the love story began."

Prior to turning his skills to bike building, James had a career in fashion, during which he began to focus on simplification as a way of evolving processes and products. In doing so, he took a sabbatical to study sustainable leadership due to having a moral crisis in relationship to the fashion industry. Sustainable leadership led him to consulting with companies around repurposing toward more-sustainable products and business models. James's commitment to being part of the sustainability solution continued when he turned his bicycle-building hobby into a small business.

James says his love of building bespoke bikes involves "a very handmade process" and doesn't use many big machines. Instead, files are the core of his work: "I have a growing collection, from big, rough bastard files for getting a rough miter started, through to using specialist files, which my youngest daughter, studying jewelry design in Pforzheim, introduced me to. And then there's my dear friend Mareck from Arco Bici, who gives me a file every time we meet—cheers, mate!"

James's workshop, at the rear of his property, has big glass windows looking over a garden where Levy, his dog, hangs out. James says, "As [I am] a lone worker, Levy provides companionship and a good excuse to get outside and take in some fresh air." His collaborations with painters, machinists, other craft people, and clients not only energize and inspire James but, as he says, "stops me becoming a hermit."

Collaborations between James and his clients, to fulfill their cycling dreams, make bike building a truly exciting experience: "Building something that fits their body and soul, whatever their cycling aspirations." James admits to being extremely competitive when he was younger but has grown to appreciate the spiritual side of cycling. As a result, he is not fixed into specific cycling genres and enjoys new projects that challenge his design curiosities.

The rodeo trout head badge. *Courtesy of Adam Gasson*

The KIS rear end, with wrap overstays, keeps things simple and has plenty of space for big rubber. *Courtesy of Adam Gasson*

Always being fascinated with how things were made, James says his design influences were forged at an early age: "I look at an object and imagine how it is put together, and how I would make and improve it." Along with this fascination, daily life and color provide James with important sources of inspiration. For example, the landscape and environment of the Yorkshire moors and dales are "wet and muddy most of the time, so even a fancy road bike must be pragmatic and functional. Stopping at the roadside with a broken bike isn't fun." His approach to design is also juxtaposed to what James refers to as "the turbo capitalistic society we are all part of[, which] tends to create complexity and innovation without real benefit. Read *Design for the Real World* by Victor Papanek, and you get where I am coming from."

James says he has enjoyed many amazing, painful, refreshing experiences on and around bicycles. One such adventure he recalls was a combination of both the best and worst cycling experience, due to unexpected weather changes:

> It was a virgin outing on a mountain bike over the Pennine Way at the very beginning of the nineties with Big Jim, an old mate. Simple ride up to the moors, turn left on the Pennine Way, and head towards Holme Moss. A day I thought I might die, laughed myself rough, and got mud in every orifice of my body. Several hours after starting, we crawled home so exhausted, had a bath, and just slept for fourteen hours! I learnt the value of planning and preparation!

When not building or having adventures on bikes, James says, "It sounds cheesy; I'm living! Life involves enjoying my wife and our young adult kids as they start their own life journeys. Cooking is my other great passion. There's nothing better than a dining table full of hungry family and friends. And of course, riding bikes, although at a leisurely pace these days!"

Jack the lad. *Courtesy of Adam Gasson*

The Rat Racer. *Courtesy of Johannes Herden*

Raw finish with hand-drawn graphics. Ride or die!
Courtesy of Johannes Herden

Trout and about roadside. *Courtesy of Finnbar Trout Cycles*

Another Jack the lad, lugged all-roader somewhere in Scandinavia, lost in the adventure: Freedom! *Courtesy of Finnbar Trout Cycles*

Steel is surreal! From Eroica special to road plus.
Courtesy of Finnbar Trout Cycles

The Comfort racer project for journalist Tim Farin.
Courtesy of Finnbar Trout Cycles

The proof is in the pudding! Tim hammers the cobbles at the amateur Tour of Flanders! *Courtesy of Finnbar Trout Cycles*

GOODDAY BIKEWORKS

GUNNISON, COLORADO, US

Chris Besnia's connection to bikes is part of his DNA. As he says, "Bikes have been a part of my identity longer than I've been a conscious being." He doesn't remember learning to ride a bike; he just knew that riding them was something he'd always wanted to do. As young boys, he and his brother loved racing their BMX bikes in the woods behind their house, located in the Berkshire Mountains of western Massachusetts. In their teenage years, they bought mountain bikes and started building pirate bike trails. Then, at sixteen, Chris got his first job at a bike shop 10 miles from his house, commuting back and forth on a road bike. Then when he moved out west to Salt Lake City, he didn't own a car for the better part of a decade. Chris says, "Riding bikes was never a political act for me; it was just part of who I am and how I got places."

Having worked in bike shops since he was sixteen, Chris thought his work trajectory was going to be a bike mechanic in the summer, work at a ski shop in the winter, and be a hobby bike builder on the side. However, he says, "At the age of thirty-five I was ready to be my own boss, and so was my girlfriend." They took a leap and opened their own frame-building/bag-making shop, with funds raised through a Kickstarter campaign during the COVID-19 pandemic. Chris says, "Sometimes I can't believe that I'm here, doing what I love and what I'm good at. I feel like a magician every time I take a few tubes and turn it into an elegant and capable machine."

Chris climbing up through Crested Butte's legendary wildflowers. *Courtesy of Tory Powers*

When Chris established Goodday Bikeworks, he wanted to create a bike that didn't exist yet. Bikes that had the handmade and artistic sensibilities of nineteenth- and early-twentieth-century bicycle manufacturing—curvaceous lines, integrated components, hand-painted finishes—but with modern geometry and components." As his frame-building and cycling interests evolved, Chris realized that the front triangle of a bike could be optimized for bike packing, so he began pushing the volume of the front triangle on the basis of standover and an elongating wheelbase: "It opened the door to slacker geometry—steeper seat tube angles and a longer front center. This makes for better climbing and descending capabilities." Thus, his favorite bike part is a dropper post.

You know when you have arrived. *Courtesy of Tory Powers*

Goodday Bikes entered a new niche when Chris's girlfriend began making artful, custom frame packs for their bikes. While they work as independent collaborators, they come together to create a design, a story, and color scheme for each bike in their shared space. Decorated with vintage bike posters, as well as vintage mountain bike and Columbia memorabilia, the custom frame packs are made up front, and Chris has his frame-building operation in the garage in the back. It is a one-stop shop: "My shop is part machining and welding, and I have a paint booth, sandblasting cabinet, and oven, as I do my own powder coating." Chris says that although he's known for making road bikes, touring bikes, gravel bikes, and mountain bikes, "I am now known for making highly specialized bike-packing rigs."

Chris's design influences are a combination of historical and environmental elements. First, it's significant that the oldest bicycle manufacturer in the US—the Columbia Bicycle Factory in Westfield, Massachusetts, was in his backyard when growing up: "That nostalgic look of late-eighteenth-, early-nineteenth-century paperboy bikes are part of the DNA of Goodday Bikes." Second, he lives and works down the road from Crested Butte, which he says "is steeped in mountain bike history, including the Pearl Pass Klunker tour." Chris explains that "a revolutionary group of rascals took these prewar paperboy bikes and modified them with motorcycle components and created the 'klunker.' My bikes are basically modern klunkers built purposely for mountain biking and bike packing." The biking opportunities in the Gunnison Valley are numerous and rugged, so his personal bikes are molded around the demands of his backyard: "I make a 'Crested Butte Hard Tail,' universally known as an 'enduro hard tail,' which utilizes a long travel fork (150 mm), steep seat tube angles (76 degrees) a 170 mm dropper post, and plus-sized tires."

Chris Besnia firing up the torch. *Courtesy of Tory Powers*

Every bike Chris builds is designed for a specific terrain. For example, "if you live in Texas and mainly ride cross-country trails in the hill country, that is what we'll tailor your bike for." For one of his customers, who has a collection of high-end and custom handbuilt bikes, Chris built a long-travel single-speed hard tail: "He calls me every week to tell me how much he loves his bike, how much attention he gets on the trail, how he's cleared features he'd never ridden before, and how he hasn't touched any of his other bikes since he got a Goodday." Though, Chris is quick to point out, "Granted, these are many of the comments I get from all my customers, but he, by far, is the most persistent with his gratitude and admiration."

When he's not building bikes for Goodday customers, Chris can be found gravel mountain biking or taking an overnight bike-packing trip in his own backyard wilderness: "During the long Colorado winter, you can find me lake skating or skiing."

Chris catching air while out for a bike pack in nearby southern Utah. *Courtesy of Neil Beltchenko*

Columbia bicycles were the backdrop of Chris's childhood. *Courtesy of Arly Landry*

A cross-country hard tail with a raw to purple powder coat. *Courtesy of Arly Landry*.

A single-speed hard tail that became a bike collector's favorite. *Courtesy of Chris Besnia*

The show bike for the 2023 MADE Bike Show, "Where the Buffalo Roam." *Courtesy of Miles Arbor*

Details of the triple triangle on a Flaming Lips–inspired road bike. *Courtesy of Arly Landry*

One of Chris's bike-packing inventions, the Spacer Cradle, protects cables and cleans up the cockpit. *Courtesy of John Watson*

HUTCHINSON
KRAKEN
KRAKEN

HUHN CYCLES

BISCHOFSGRÜN, GERMANY

Ralf Holleis is captivated by the dynamic combination of the simplicity and intricate craftsmanship of bikes. This presents a fascinating paradox: A bike's design may appear simple, but each detail is a complex marvel of engineering. Ralf says, "The elegance lies in their timeless design—while the fundamental concept has remained relatively unchanged for fifty years, the meticulous execution of every detail evolves and improves with each passing year." Ralf's relationship with bikes and the origin of his brand are firmly anchored in his childhood. Bikes were his first gateway to freedom, long before holding a driver's license: "From an emotional standpoint, bikes symbolize the purest form of liberation, a feeling that transcends generations." Besides an early visceral connection to bikes, Ralf's hands-on bike skills were honed experimenting with bikes in his father's workshop. "I vividly recall cutting old bikes apart and welding them back together in unconventional ways," he says.

It wasn't until his university years that Ralf began to delve deeper into the art of frame building, which culminated in a thesis on an innovative track bike named the Vorwaertz (VRZ). As he notes, "It was the world's pioneer in utilizing additive manufacturing (3-D printing) for frame components, specifically titanium lugs bonded together with carbon tubes. He takes some pride in recognizing early on the enormous potential of 3-D-printed metal for small bike brands and frame builders: "Over the years, I've shared my knowledge with any frame builder who sought guidance,

Moorhuhn build, with 100% European-made parts.
Courtesy of Ralf Holleis Dipl. Industrial Designer

and it's immensely gratifying to see that 3-D printing has become a common practice in the frame-building community." For example, he received a message from Bastion, an Australian boutique bike brand, saying he had inspired their bike construction. He says, "This not only brought a smile to my face but highlighted the collaborative and inspirational spirit within the bike-building community." Over time, Ralf's focus shifted toward sustainability: "This led me to eliminate carbon from my frame constructions." Today, Ralf's passion lies in crafting mountain bikes primarily from steel or titanium, combining innovation with a commitment to environmentally conscious materials.

Ralf is a lone craftsman, working from a one-hundred-year-old shed he and his wife, Andrea, meticulously renovated. The bespoke shed seamlessly combines Ralf's workspace with the living quarters, which, Ralf says, "exudes a small, yet cozy, ambiance." The real charm of his workspace lies in the amalgamation of Old World craftsmanship and modern technology. It's adorned with a carefully curated selection of vintage machines that carry the echoes of the past. Alongside these stand modern marvels such as his FDM 3-D printer and the handheld CNC (computerized numerical control) machine, the Shaper Origin: "This fusion of the traditional and the contemporary not only defines my workspace but also reflects the essence of my craft—a harmonious blend of time-honored techniques and cutting-edge innovation." Of all his tools, he says his heart belongs to the lathe. He says, "There's something almost magical about using this forty-year-old machine to transform raw metal into the precise shapes needed for a bike. It's more than just a tool; it's a conduit for turning imagination into tangible, rideable art."

Ralf also opens the Huhn Cycles workshop to people keen to learn bike building. He particularly remembers two eager young enthusiasts: "Watching their eyes light up as they fashioned their own bicycles was incredibly rewarding. The real magic happened when we embarked on that first ride together, a shared adventure born from a labor of love. It's moments like these that underscore the true essence of building bikes—a journey that extends far beyond the workshop and into the realm of shared passion and camaraderie."

Ralf likes the delicate dance between engineering precision and emotive design. As he says, "Building a bike is not just assembling parts; it's about creating a functional and emotional masterpiece, where every detail speaks to the rider's heart while meeting the highest standards of engineering excellence. It's a harmonious fusion of form and function, where every curve and component serve a purpose beyond the aesthetic." He says this is particularly true of the dropout, his absolute favorite component, which holds a paradoxical charm: "It's the most intelligent component on a bike, a testament to timeless principles that haven't changed for decades. The dropout, for me, is where the entire design process begins and, simultaneously, concludes. It embodies the essence of contemporary design within a framework of enduring tradition."

VRZ: 3-D-printed titanium lugs get removed from the building plate. *Courtesy of Ralf Holleis Dipl. Industrial Designer*

Likewise, Ralf says that his cradle of inspiration and ideas "is undeniably the saddle of a bike, particularly during the contemplative moments of pedaling uphill. It's a time-consuming endeavor that allows my thoughts to wander freely." Technological advancements and production processes, both modern and historical, also provide a wellspring of inspiration. For example, Ralf acknowledges that he's fascinated by the ingenuity behind the mass production of lugged bicycle frames, for their accessibility to a broader audience.

Ralf's design influences "span a spectrum from the sleek lines of modern architecture to the timeless creations of midcentury furniture designers." Even the rugged aesthetics of old motorbikes serve as a nostalgic muse, as well as where he has lived and worked. During his university days in the city, he was immersed in the vibrant fixie scene and crafted the VRZ track bike, ideal for urban commuting: "Now, life has led me to the mountains, where my daily joy revolves around navigating single trails." Living in Bischofsgrün has turned him into a mountain-biking enthusiast, which has led him to specialize in building mountain bikes: "My commitment is to enhance them constantly, drawing from personal experiences on the trails to make each bike better than the last."

Ralf finds immense satisfaction and comfort in his chosen profession. While he entertained the idea of becoming an architect, he ultimately chose the path of industrial design and bike building and has never looked back. As an industrial designer, Ralf focuses on creating kids' furniture, buggies, and various other products. He says, "In my free time, I love hitting the mountain bike trails in Fichtelgebirge. But the most fulfilling part of my life is spending time with my wife and our two-year-old daughter."

Ralf Holleis portrait with the VRZ. *Courtesy of Jörg Spaniol*

The VRZ titanium lugs, tin-coated before glueing. *Courtesy of Ralf Holleis Dipl. Industrial Designer*

The VRZ build in pieces. *Courtesy of Ralf Holleis Dipl. Industrial Designer*

VRZ: the world's first bike using 3-D-printed lugs to construct a lightweight frame structure.
Courtesy of Ralf Holleis Dipl. Industrial Designer

Moorhuhn lugs, 3-D-printed stainless steel.
Courtesy of Pietro Borra

Moorhuhn finishing process. *Courtesy of Ralf Holleis Dipl. Industrial Designer*

Moorhuhn lugs coming out of the 3-D printer.
Courtesy of Ralf Holleis Dipl. Industrial Designer

The Moorhuhn TI European build.
Courtesy of Lars Scharl

GRAVEL SPEEDERO

ICHNU CYCLES

SERRAMANNA, ITALY

Fabio Putzolu says, "Bicycles have such a timeless beauty and stand as a true expression of humankind's smartness." In 2011, after working in the communication and advertising industry, Fabio realized that the advertising industry was not fulfilling his aspirations. He came from a family of cyclists, and as his passion for bicycles grew, by 2012 Fabio began designing his first bikes under the brand name of Fabike. As he explains, "They were designed by me and made in Asia," which became unsustainable during the COVID-19 pandemic.

Fabio responded by turning his attention to becoming independent from external suppliers, by making as much as possible in-house or sourcing parts locally. ICHNU Cycles was the result. He chose the name Ichnu as a derivation of Ichnusa, the ancient name of Sardinia, his birthplace and where he grew up. He wanted not only to make stunning bikes using technology and innovation, but to make high-end bikes more durable and, therefore, more sustainable. In 2023, a prototype of the first ICHNU frame, the ERA, was exhibited at the Bespoked bike show in Dresden, Germany. He says, "When I started making everything in-house, I realized I was no longer just a creative, but I became a creator. The ability to make beautiful things happen by your own means is something that gives a satisfaction difficult to explain. It just makes me feel alive."

The ICHNU ERA, presented during Bespoked 2023.
Courtesy of Adam Gasson

Fabio creates his bikes in a former screen-printing workspace, which, coincidentally, was the very same workspace where he got his first job after he graduated from studying design and advertising. He mostly works alone but from time to time has some people helping with the manual work, and others supporting him with the engineering of the frames. As he points out, "I'm quite proud of the technology that I have developed to merge carbon fiber with Dyneema fiber. This allows me to create the filament-winding tubes that I use for my ICHNU ERA."

For design inspiration, Fabio admits to being a bit of an innovation nerd: "I try always to look for new technical solutions, new designs, and new production improvements. For this reason, I always look at cutting-edge innovations, which are sometimes found outside the bike industry." He also reads a lot about materials and new technologies, browses design magazines, and talks as much as possible to other innovators, including people working in the digital industry. "In the end, what matters is not the product you create but the approach you have towards it," he says.

According to Fabio, "Sardinia has not had a great cycling culture, but lately things have been changing. Sardinia is becoming a true cycling destination for people all over the world. I feel I could be part of this change, supporting other local businesses and passionate people to make the local more global. It feels I'm giving back to my island." This passion for bikes and cycling goes both ways, with some of Fabio's customers sharing their passion with him. He says, "I have a Belgian guy who bought a bike from me several years ago. He regularly sends a photo every month of him, his bike, and his dog."

Apart from creating bikes under his ICHNU brand, Fabio has a dream. As a self-confessed "traveling maniac, almost a nomad," he would also like to keep traveling to experience different places and ways of living: "I have a dream that one day I will be able to make my business a nomad/itinerant business and bring my workshop around the world with me. I have some ideas . . . let's see if it will ever happen."

Titanium 3-D-printed bottom bracket.
Courtesy of ICHNU Cycles

Opposite: The ICHNU ERA, presented during Bespoked 2023.
Courtesy of Adam Gasson

Titanium 3-D-printed dropouts. *Courtesy of ICHNU Cycles*

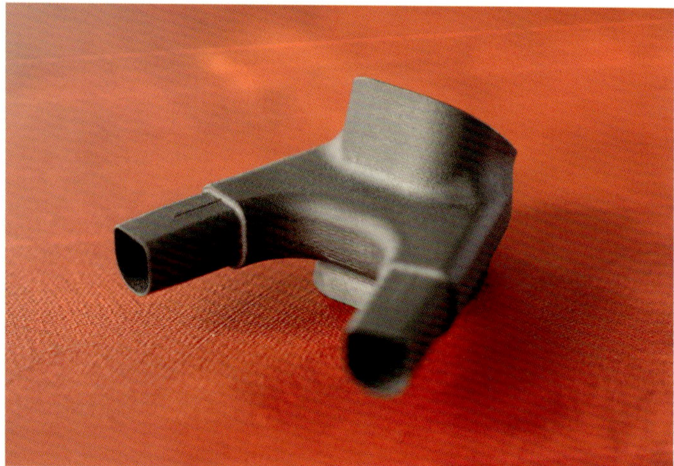

Titanium 3-D-printed seat tube and seat stay junction. *Courtesy of ICHNU Cycles*

First ride ever of the ICHNU ERA. *Courtesy of ICHNU Cycles*

who today would ride
on 'square' wheels?
take the rough like the
smooth on a Moulton
the new bicycle with the
revolutionary rubber
suspension system
Moulton

MOULTON BICYCLE COMPANY

BRADFORD-ON-AVON, UK

Dan Farrell, part of the Moulton team, gives us a window into Moulton's history and workings, and his viewpoints. Dan recalls reading this quote—"Bicycles are the seven-league boots of the modern age." In his opinion, those words explain exactly how riding a bike feels:

> If we walk, we can cover 10 or 20 miles per day, and we pass through the landscape slowly. Yet, if we use a bicycle, the (seemingly) simple mechanical device that it is, our progress can be an order of magnitude farther and faster, despite the "engine" being the same heart, lungs, and legs.

The bicycle is almost magical! Dan also references author and journalist Twells Brex, who once wrote, "This slender, whippet thing of steel and rubber that carries a man far and fast, by his own glad effort, on the open road and takes him away from his cares . . . as nothing can."

Dan notes that while the Moulton Bicycle Company story starts in 1840s, when Stephen Moulton brought Charles Goodyear's vulcanized rubber to Europe, Alex Moulton's introduction to bicycles came during the 1956 Suez Crisis, when he borrowed a bicycle as "a serious alternative means of locomotion"—to eke out his petrol ration. Dan says, "Alex found 'a revelation of joy' in riding this lightweight curly Hetchins but found it inconvenient as a practical vehicle. His resolve to improve on it resulted in the original Moulton bicycle of 1962." This pivotal moment pioneered the small-wheeled, open-frame architecture that all Moulton bicycles (and many others) have followed ever since. This design also brought in full-suspension for comfort and road holding, a key tenet of Moulton bicycles. Dan states, "Revolutionary at launch, the Moulton enjoyed great success, and Raleigh bought Moulton's business in 1967. Manufacture in Nottingham continued until 1974, after which Alex decided to go it alone and took a conscious decision to eschew volume production and design high-quality performance bicycles for discerning owners. This, of course, is what Moulton still does to this day."

In Dan's opinion, Moulton is a unique business for two reasons: "We are lucky to have a group of people dedicated to continuing the work of Alex Moulton. Many have been here for a long time—in one case over sixty years." The Moulton factory in Bradford-on-Avon, Wiltshire, is equally unique, with its center being a Scottish baronial-style stable block, complete with a round tower: "The technical office is in a seventeenth-century farm building, and the main office is a 1960s timber-and-stone creation, very much of the Frank Lloyd Wright idiom. We also now have the original 1962 Moulton bicycle factory, which is facilitating expansion of the business to meet increased demand. All of this is wrapped up within the grounds of Alex Moulton's Jacobean mansion—the Hall, a fine landscaped garden with stone summer houses and magnificent specimen trees. We build and paint our frames and assemble our bicycles here, so we are all 'at the coal face' and can discuss matters of design and manufacture easily and effectively."

Original Moulton Bicycles brochure, 1962.
Courtesy of Moulton Bicycle Company

There is always a desire—a challenge—to make something function better, weigh less, become more elegant. As Dan notes, Alex Moulton would speak of "wanting something to be more pleasing to own and to use." Much of the excitement comes from problem-solving, sketching, cutting metal—through to testing and using: "Because we do so much ourselves, on-site, this can sometimes happen very quickly, further adding to the magic."

Dan's design influences are many and varied: "Aside from Moulton's extensive back catalog, I do take an interest in efficient structures appearing elsewhere—aeroplanes, boats, and bridges. Aircraft have an aerodynamic efficiency forced upon them, and I find the resulting aesthetic appealing. Similarly, civil and naval architecture give us good examples (and bad ones) of geometry and proportion. Whilst I often cannot agree with 'If it looks right, it is right,' the opposite is certainly true." Since Moulton's history runs deep, any design inspiration brings great responsibility. As Dan points out, "We have carefully defined what the Moulton bicycle is, and we usually keep within these parameters; certainly, we only step outside them with full knowledge and due care."

At Moulton there is a reason for everything in design and engineering. These reasons are varied, and often not obvious - and they may relate to areas such as ease of servicing or transportation rather than the performance of the bicycle itself. With such an extensive history, the question "what is the reason for this?" is often asked, safe in the knowledge that there is an answer, even if it takes a bit of research to find it. Times change, of course, and sometimes the justification of design decisions changes with it - Moulton's method was to question these decisions and take advantage of technological progress to make better bicycles. We don't ride high-wheelers anymore!

When it comes to choosing a favorite bike component, Dan has a weakness for 1980s Campagnolo, particularly the first-series C-Record: "One could argue (very successfully) that modern components are functionally superior, but the elegance and polish of Vicenza's production of this era remains unmatched. At times the mechanics seemed needlessly idiosyncratic, but amongst this lay [*sic*] some real gems that should have gained wider acceptance much earlier than they did. Add to this the beautiful packaging and the mystique of Campagnolo never using model name labels . . . modern components seem to be lacking in soul."

The Moulton AM—the advanced engineering bicycle.
Courtesy of Moulton Bicycle Company

Dan also likes simple tools that work well, such as Rixen & Kaul's Spokey and Park's Rescue Wrench (the latter being the modern-day dumbbell spanner).

Having worked in the cycle industry for thirty years, Dan honestly cannot remember seriously considering doing anything else. Although there have been times when others have tried to tempt him away into other design engineering jobs, he says, "Ultimately the thing about Moulton is that it is such a great product, such a fantastic bicycle."

Working at Moulton has also dragged Dan into historical writing and research, as well as being involved with the Institution of Engineering Designers and the British Standards Institution. These activities, along with messing around with boats (at one stage, having lived on one for sixteen years), old cars, and other mechanical things, occupy Dan's time when he's not working with or riding bicycles.

AM-ATB—the world's first production full-suspension mountain bike (1988). *Courtesy of Dan Farrell, Moulton Bicycle Company*

Stainless steel—the Moulton AM GT. *Courtesy of Dan Farrell, Moulton Bicycle Company*

Alex Moulton—innovative engineer. *Courtesy of George Llewellyn*

Brazing in the Moulton Factory. *Courtesy of Dan Farrell, Moulton Bicycle Company*

Moulton Earl Grey 1866. *Courtesy of Dan Farrell, Moulton Bicycle Company*

Moulton Earl Grey 1866, separated for storage or transportation. *Courtesy of Dan Farrell, Moulton Bicycle Company*

The Hall, Bradford-on-Avon. *Courtesy of Dan Farrell, Moulton Bicycle Company*

Moulton Jubilee (on the grounds of the Hall). *Courtesy of Dan Farrell, Moulton Bicycle Company*

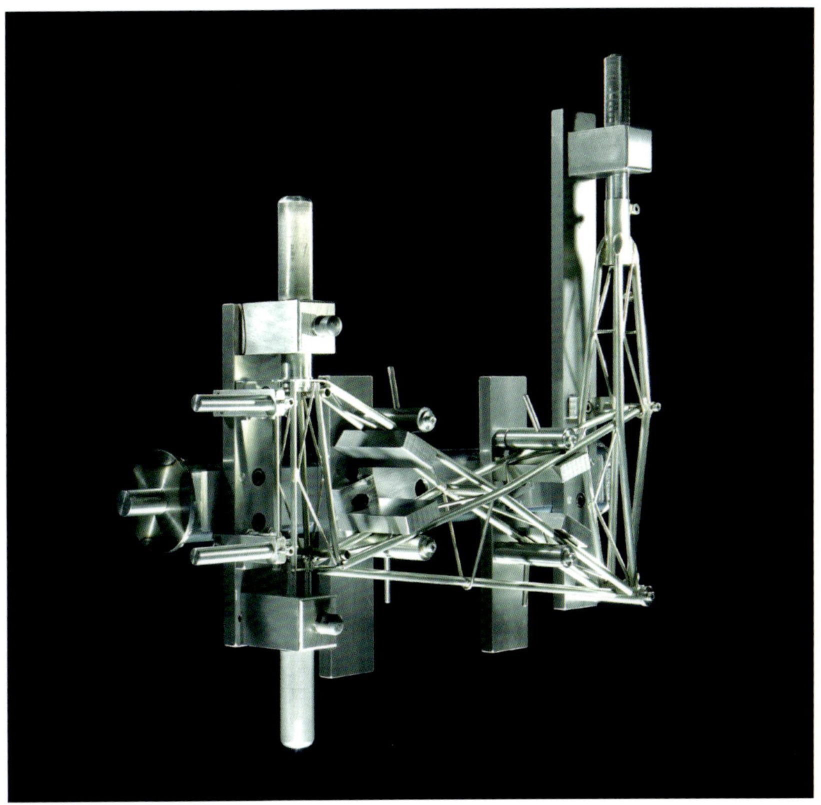

Moulton New Series CENTURY bicycle, shown in front of the Moulton Bicycle Factory. *Courtesy of Dan Farrell, Moulton Bicycle Company*

Moulton New Series frame jig—all jigs and fixtures are made in-house at Bradford-on-Avon. *Courtesy of Robert Smith*

Moulton New Series SAFARI—the next generation of Moulton bicycles. *Courtesy of Dan Farrell, Moulton Bicycle Company*

The Moulton Sales & Marketing team in the 1960s—David Duffield, John Unsworth, Lloyd Binch. Alex Moulton was closely involved with the design of the Mini and used them to great effect as company vehicles. *Courtesy of Moulton Bicycle Company*

Original Series 1 Moulton Bicycle general arrangement drawing, 1962. *Courtesy of Moulton Bicycle Company*

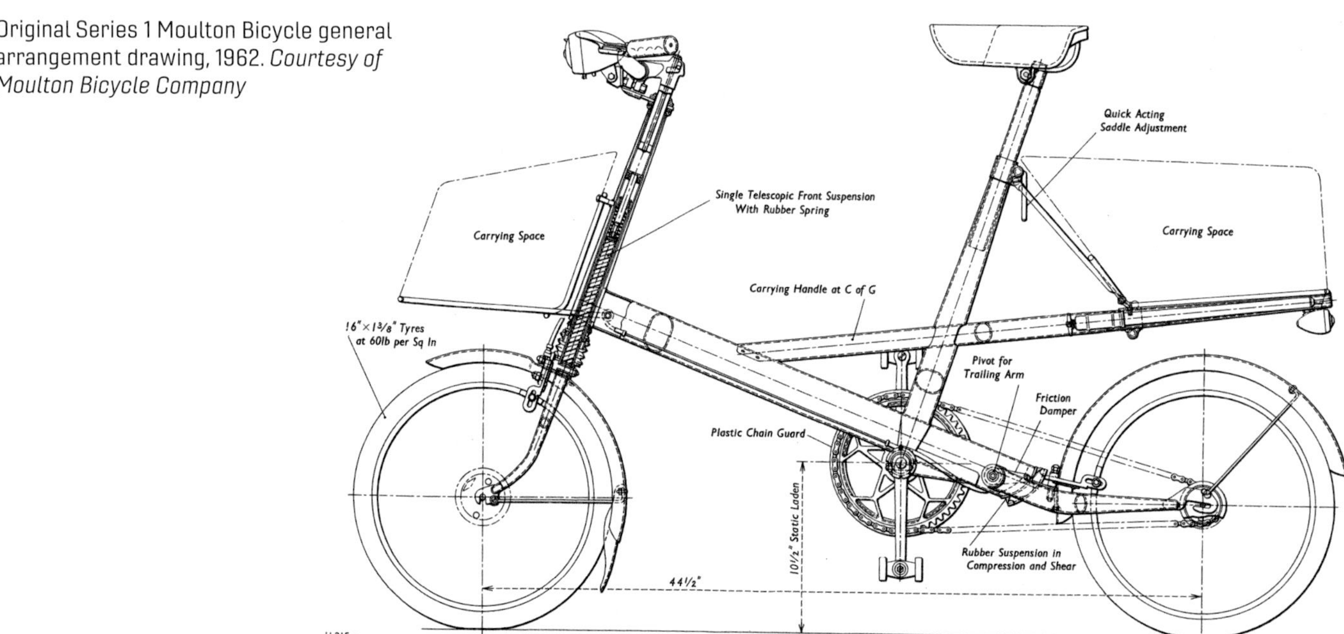

Moulton TSR space-frame bicycle. *Courtesy of Dan Farrell, Moulton Bicycle Company*

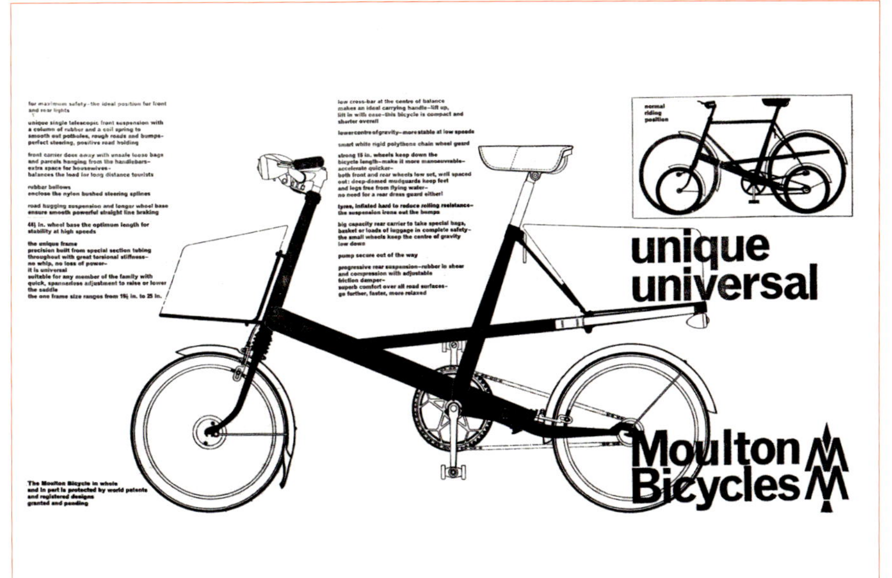

The original Moulton bicycle was unique, universal—and revolutionary—when it was launched in 1962. *Courtesy of Moulton Bicycle Company*

Moulton bicycles have been used in competitive events for many years, with one of the most famous achievements being Jim Glover's world speed record in 1986—a record that still stands to this day. *Courtesy of Moulton Bicycle Company*

NAKED BICYCLES AND DESIGN

QUADRA ISLAND, BRITISH COLUMBIA, CANADA

Sam has a bike mantra: "Bikes are the perfect distillation of form and function. They are simple to make and to ride, but it takes a lifetime of play to master both. Bike building is a chance to create for someone an object that is beautiful on its own but also beautifully reflects the essence of its rider and of its builder. The conversation that happens when builder and rider come together in the creation of a bicycle can be pure, distilled, and easily recognized joy."

Sam Whittingham originally trained and worked as a stage designer. But traveling for work was hard on family life, and so his original passion for bicycles made sense in the end. Sam started Naked Bicycles and Design in 1999, fueled by pure whimsy and asking a simple question: "Can I make a bicycle with just a few tools?" Sam believes that a good bicycle has no more or fewer parts or ornamentation than is required for the adventure desired of it. This is one of the reasons that Sam and his team build exclusively in titanium—no paint, no rust, and extremely light and durable. Sam likes to say, "We build with unicorn bones!"

Naked Bicycles has almost always been two or three people, including Sam. This helps keep the brand moving forward with fresh ideas, enthusiasm, and a sense of teamwork. Sam says, "Having this number of people allows clients to truly have a personalized experience, where the same person that fit them also designed, welded, and finished the bicycle for them." There is a simple creative joy from using very few tools and materials to bring someone's dreams to adventurous reality. Sam says, "Watching a smiling client ride into their first of many adventures, full of anticipation and energy, never loses its charm. Bicycles are wings for the soul. Who wouldn't want to try to give that to another being?"

After twenty-five years of building, the basic tools and skills are second nature, and no one tool or process of actual fabrication really stands out. Each task is unique but part of a very satisfying whole. The real chance for creativity and thought comes in the design process. This is where Sam focuses his attention these days. He believes that very few people really understand how a bicycle and rider move through space: "I am most excited when I find real insight from experimentation, experience, and research over many years, to cut through the jargon of popular geometry and fitting misconceptions to find the real nuggets of driving parameters that will result in that magic-carpet feeling we all look for in our bicycle-riding experience."

To Sam, fitting is simply a matter of finding those points in space where you will touch the bicycle. Handling is simply a matter of where you are in space in relation to where the bicycle touches the ground. "When these fit and handling numbers work in harmony with the ever-changing dynamics of the environment, previous biases, and our physical-control inputs, then we have found the magic sauce." It is also an error to think of these numbers as static. They need to be in constant change and flow out of necessity. As Einstein said, "To keep your balance, you must keep moving!" How do we find these numbers? According to Sam, "That's the never-ending quest that I love. If you don't dive in and continue to ask the basic questions of how

Sam Wittingham. *Courtesy of Kari Medig*

naked
TERAVAIL
TERAVAIL

the heck a bike stays upright and makes you feel a certain way when you ride it, then your only option would be to blindly copy what has been done by others, who have likely just copied others themselves. That's not design; that's forgery."

As much as possible, Sam looks for inspirations outside the bicycle world: "There are so many amazing sources to draw from, including nature, architecture, art, and especially other crafts." Not least, where he lives: "I live at the end of a road, on a small island, several ferries from a major center. We are deep in the British Columbia rainforest, with miles and miles of rugged roads and vibrant single-track. It is the perfect playground for adventure. Every bicycle we build is against this backdrop of daily living, and that gets alloyed into the titanium."

Sam relies on play, experiment, and "happy accidents" as well. People can forget that some of the best things are learned or created from just mucking around with tools and media we have on hand. To study movement and fit, Sam is more inspired by dancers, other athletics, and even some animals for a truly dynamic understanding of bodies moving through space. "I find this type of lateral thinking much more creative, and even if we come back around to something seemingly traditional, we at least have the awareness of why we arrived at our choices," he says.

Bike shows also provide sources of inspiration, comradeship, and friendly competition for most bike builders. Sam recalls a heartfelt story that led to a famous happenstance at a bike show with a touching outcome:

> In 2007, Peter, a very dear friend of mine got cancer and passed away in a matter of weeks in the middle of guiding a bike trip. He was a larger-than-life character, with an immense heart that left a big hole in the world, and it affected me greatly. I stopped everything else I was building and retreated into my workshop for a month and built an unusual bike in his honor, which I then took to NAHBS [North American Handmade Bike Show]. I had no idea how this strange machine would be received. It ended up taking home top honors for Best in Show, People's Choice, and President's Choice. Something that has never been repeated. It was purchased by Lance Armstrong to be the centerpiece of his new shop at the time in Austin, Texas. This story may have lost some of its shine, given Lance's public history, but there is a little extra nuance I carry with me. When I told Lance the genesis story of the bike and Peter's sudden death from cancer, he quietly funded the same amount he had paid for the bike, to help cover Peter's daughter's future schooling. This is a reminder that no one is just one thing. We all have many stories that define us.

Beyond bikes, Sam loves trail building: "Right out my door is an amazing Lego box of rocks, soil, mountains, water, and trees to play with. Designing new ribbons of single-track and working the ever-changing landscape of older trails out in the woods gives such a strong connection to the environment and teaches us to work with landscape, not against it. I have a voracious appetite for philosophy and find great insight from the awareness that comes from regular meditation practice."

A couple of pedal strokes from Naked HQ on Quadra Island, British Columbia, is a vast ribbon of single-track.
Courtesy of Naked Bicycles

Sam Whittingham carving "unicorn bones" in his Naked HQ workshop.
Courtesy of Kari Medig

A Naked Bicycle is in a constant state of wanderlust. *Courtesy of Naked Bicycles*

Naked Bicycles in repose off the west coast of Vancouver Island. *Courtesy of Naked Bicycles*

That rare moment when just before a new Naked Bike springs forth into a life of adventure. *Courtesy of Naked Bicycles*

Naked Bike owners such as Lyle often become lifelong friends. *Courtesy of Naked Bicycles*

Naked Factory Racing national champion and world cup racer Emily Johnson. *Courtesy of Naked Bicycles*

Naked Bicycles are welded with love, logic, and elbow grease. *Courtesy of Naked Bicycles*

Naked summer romance. *Courtesy of Naked Bicycles*

Anodized-titanium Unicorn spotted in the wild. *Courtesy of Naked Bicycles*

Naked Bicycles born and thriving in the rainforests of British Columbia. *Courtesy of Naked Bicycles*

Opposite: What's better than a Naked KISS (Keep It Single Speed) on Valentine's Day? *Courtesy of Naked Bicycles*

naked
34
FOX
TURBINE

PARLEE
FORCE

PARLEE CYCLES

BEVERLY, MASSACHUSETTS, US

Parlee Cycles was founded in 2000 by Bob Parlee, an enthusiastic cyclist who had over twenty years' experience building high-performance boats. While working on race boats, Bob saw the potential of carbon fiber composites and brought his composite expertise to bikes. Since 2000, Parlee has exclusively worked with composites and is renowned for custom geometry carbon bikes. According to Parlee, they were among the first brands to "tame" the performance of composites and create high-performance bicycles that were also comfortable: "That has been our signature ever since. Performance and comfort from one bike!" Above all, when it comes to answering the question "Why bikes?," the Parlee team says, "It's simple. It's a love affair. Bikes are everything to us. Bikes are incredibly elegant and honest machines. They are fun to ride, are great for your health, bring people together, and are great for the planet. What's not to love?"

The small Parlee team comprises CEO John Harrison, who joined them in 2023, and the design and custom fabrication team, of Tom Rodi, Lyndall Robinson, Rommel Mariano, and Cody Haight, who works in their self-described world-class custom paint department known as the Parlee Paint Lab. With Tom joining Parlee in 2003, Rommel in 2005, and Lyndall in 2015, "there are decades of experience within the team." Sadly, their founder, Bob Parlee, who headed up the design and custom fabrication team as chief designer, passed away in September 2024.

The Parlee team works in a wonderful, sunlit space in Beverly, Massachusetts, which houses their design and custom fabrication: "For us, because we work only with composites and do all our own design and fabrication, each design is a clean slate." That is, they are not starting with existing tubes. They design the shapes, make the parts, and manufacture them on-site to perform exactly how they want them to. This is something they believe is really special and truly unique in the industry: "It's incredible to go from a roll of fabric on a Monday morning and have a rideable frame by Wednesday dinnertime!" They also make the point that carbon composites are unique because there are no training courses, textbooks, or canned solutions for building bikes: "You must figure things out for yourself; 95 percent of our tools and molds are designed by our staff and built just for us for one special task. There's a great satisfaction from building a bike with tools that you have designed and made yourself." Apart from their handmade tools, the team loves the classic Campagnolo T wrench from the Campagnolo tool kit: "Tullio probably spins in his grave when he sees us using it on through-axles, but it works great for those, and the 8 mm end is great for our bottle cage hardware. It's just satisfying sometimes to use a tool that is fifty or sixty years old on a modern bike."

Parlee's early bicycle designs were naturally influenced by boats, since they wanted to have practical, elegant, and durable designs. The aerospace and automotive industries also provide plenty of inspiration to designers. But, of course, "inspiration is everywhere around you if you open your eyes, ears, and mind. Humans have been designing objects and tools forever." Accordingly, the team says their bikes are often

Fall in New England and a Parlee gravel bike are a fantastic combination. *Courtesy of Hunter Kelley, Parlee Cycles, Inc.*

influenced by nature: "Carbon composites are closer to organic materials, like wood, than most people think, so we look to nature for our shapes." Bob had a lot of experience in traditional wooden boat construction and has shared his knowledge with the team over the years: "Much like wood, carbon composites are anisotropic. Meaning different characteristics in different directions." This is why Parlee believes that carbon is the best material for building bikes, "but you must respect the materials."

Parlee acknowledges that they have been fortunate to be part of a resurgence of smaller, independent, custom-focused bicycles over the past fifteen years: "We know a lot of these builders personally and are inspired by their work too, even if it is in steel or titanium. Compared to two decades ago, there is a global community of retailers, fitters, and cyclists who now appreciate the work of smaller, more-focused brands. They don't want to buy bikes from global conglomerates. Cyclists want to have a relationship with the people who design and build their bikes. That inspires us too."

Parlee has had a fair number of well-known pro cyclists and celebrities buy their bikes. They have also created "some cool prototype projects for big companies." Though those projects are always fun, it's working with regular cyclists on their dream bikes that provides the most-satisfying moments for the Parlee team: "We're just a small group of passionate cyclists, and we are always dreaming of our next bikes the way our clients are. Speaking of dreams, a story that has always resonated with them is about someone who never gave up on one day owning their dream Parlee bike:

> Back in the day, we had a guy named Peter call us for years with endless questions about a bike, always telling us that he was saving his tips from working as a waiter in NYC for the ultimate custom bike. He was the nicest guy on the phone, who would call and give us updates on his progress and his plans, but we were never sure if he was serious. Finally, about five years later, he had saved enough money and ordered the most incredible custom road bike. His Parlee had all the best parts and an incredible custom finish. The bike paid homage to his family, who sacrificed everything so he could immigrate to the US.

Inspired by Peter, Parlee started using the hashtag #myparlee on social media: "For us and our clients, it's more than just two wheels and some parts."

As self-described problem-solvers, the Parlee design team cannot imagine doing anything else but working with bikes, and they believe there is so much more to discover: "Composite bikes are less than forty years old. Metal bikes have been around for over a hundred years. We think there is so much more to come in the next twenty-five to fifty years with composites and bikes."

Parlee's New England location has also been a big influence on the bikes they build: "What people call 'all-road' or 'gravel' bikes, now, are the type of bikes that just made sense to ride here." The area has a lot of old, rough farm roads, and the winters are brutal to the paved roads: "You need a capable, comfortable bike, and our bikes have always been both." The Parlee team feels blessed to live 5 miles from the ocean and some great outdoor spaces: "So, there's tons of other activities like sailing and hiking, but if we can be out riding, we will be!"

CEO John Harrison and custom production manager Lyndall Robinson review a new custom carbon frame at Parlee headquarters in Beverly, Massachusetts. *Courtesy of Hunter Kelley, Parlee Cycles, Inc.*

Chief designer Bob Parlee is regarded as one of the pioneers of modern carbon fiber bikes. *Courtesy of Hunter Kelley, Parlee Cycles, Inc.*

A chainstay is removed from its mold at the Parlee workshop. Parlee makes all tubes and parts for their custom bikes in-house in Beverly, Massachusetts. *Courtesy of Hunter Kelley, Parlee Cycles, Inc.*

Master frame builder Rommel Mariano has been with Parlee for nearly twenty years. No one has built more custom carbon frames than Rommel. His passion for bikes (of all kinds) is unmatched. *Courtesy of Hunter Kelley, Parlee Cycles, Inc.*

Parlee is known for the most incredible carbon work. Most carbon bikes are painted for a reason. Parlee bikes can be purchased with no paint and all the carbon work visible. *Courtesy of Hunter Kelley, Parlee Cycles, Inc.*

Detail shot of a custom Parlee gravel bike. Clean lines and amazing attention to detail have defined Parlee's work for decades. *Courtesy of Hunter Kelley, Parlee Cycles, Inc.*

Product manager Tom Rodi assembles a bike for testing. Tom has worked for Parlee since 2003. He drives the new bike design process for Parlee and is *a bit* obsessed with bikes. *Courtesy of Hunter Kelley, Parlee Cycles, Inc.*

Parlee's Paint Lab is now known as one of the best custom paint shops in North America. Customers dream it and the Paint Lab makes it happen. *Courtesy of Hunter Kelley, Parlee Cycles, Inc.*

Despite the cutting-edge carbon technology, Parlee road bikes have always had elegant proportions. *Courtesy of Hunter Kelley, Parlee Cycles, Inc.*

ERGON
PARLEE
GOODYEAR VECTOR
ZIPP
353

PROVA
DURA-ACE

PROVA CYCLES

HEIDELBERG HEIGHTS, MELBOURNE, AUSTRALIA

Prova Cycles, established in 2015, is owned and operated by siblings Mark and Kelly Hester. Their business is named after an Italian word meaning prove or demonstrate. Kelly says, "Mark always knew that something would exist as the name Prova and had earmarked it since his youth." Kelly also points out that Mark's younger years were spent spannering (also known as wrenching) and modifying race cars: "This, along with the usual country kid antics, proved to be good grounding in working with his hands."

Mark's foray into designing and building bikes began while working as a mechanical engineer in the UK and spending time at the Bicycle Academy, Frome, UK, where he built his first frames. He then built his first protypes after he and his partner moved home to Australia. "Working in an office with less [*sic*] links to the creative element of engineering work was also a big motivation to create an independent business producing the very best bikes we can," Mark says.

Kelly Hester, a chef, was looking for a change, which happened to coincide with her job being impacted by the COVID-19 pandemic. She started with Prova part-time, doing composite laminating and 3-D-printed part surface finishing. Kelly eventually moved into a full-time role, and now the brother-and-sister team share many of the tasks required to run a bicycle-manufacturing company. For Mark, bikes

Titanium Integrale build for a client in Copenhagen features our popular Brunel paint scheme in pearl white with candy-green detail. *Courtesy of Erik Son*

are the perfect outlet for combining a passion for engineering and design with the lifelong love of riding: "Making custom handmade bikes is a great opportunity to make something that people feel passionate about. It encompasses a great balance between independent working and bringing together like-minded creatives like those working in paint, bike fit, and the finishing/assembly process."

Prova's workshop is located in an old restored red-brick factory with a kitchen in the center and a timber mezzanine that adds warmth to the space. Their tailor-made workspace has allowed them to focus on lean manufacturing, utilizing knowledge both from the automotive and commercial kitchen worlds, which, Kelly says, "surprisingly have similarities!" Drawing on the benefit of working in a few different factories and creating a detailed CAD model of their machines and benches, Kelly says, "We were able to build a manufacturing space perfectly suited to the one bike a week we make." A crucial tool for Prova has become 3-D design software. "Mark's background as a design engineer enables the creation of frames that are recognizably ours and completely unique," says Kelly. This, combined with the advent of additive manufacturing, has opened up many different design solutions for the bicycle. Mark and Kelly claim that they were one of the first in the world to weld 3-D-printed structural parts into frames.

Mark and Kelly enjoying a coffee out at the front of the factory in Heidelberg Heights, not long after moving in. *Courtesy of Andy White*

Mark believes in creating bikes that clients work hard and also treat like a work of art. That is, combining desirability with the highest level of functionality and durability. Mark says, "Inspiration can be found everywhere. Being out on the bike can at times be almost meditative, and at other times it is where all the good ideas are formed." Given Mark's interest in race cars, he also takes inspiration from 1970s and '80s motorsport. According to him, this was a period of big changes

in design philosophies, aerodynamics, and materials used: "An example of this influence can be seen in our dropouts."

The most important design theory, for Mark, is to achieve even distribution of stress in the structure: "Butted tubes provide this distribution—the process of reducing the wall thickness away from the joints, thereby distributing the stress where tubes meet." He fondly recalls many conversations about this procedure with the late frame builder Ewen Gellie: "Each Prova frame we make includes custom butted titanium main tubes, made in-house." Prova regards itself as producing some of the most advanced custom titanium frames for clients around the world: "One of the first international handmade shows we attended was Bespoked Bristol 2018, where one of our bikes won best in show." Prova also received other awards at the same show and has gone on to be awarded others at subsequent shows.

Mark and Kelly feel lucky to be part of a thriving cycling scene in Melbourne and its surrounding regional areas, even sometimes running into other Prova riders: "Our commute to the factory can be on the road, gravel tracks, or single-track. Living on the edge of some of the nicest gravel riding means the Mostro probably gets the most kilometers." It's also nice to meet Prova customers who travel many kilometers on their bike: "At the 2024 Tour Down Under, we met a customer who had ridden his Prova bike across two Australian states to Adelaide for the event, and this was not the first time he had ridden to the tour."

Reflecting on the forks in the road that led to the establishment of Prova, Mark says, "Meeting the folk from the Bicycle Academy and taking time off work to build some frames for enjoyment has snowballed a little!" Then, a visit to the Bespoked Bristol show as a curious and potential buyer sparked what has become his life.

When he's not building and the bikes are on the rack, Mark Hester spends time camping or hiking with his partner or dog Ruby (or both). Kelly Hester spends time out riding with her young daughter, who rides a custom titanium 20-inch MTB!

Titanium Integrale seat lug detail in high-polish finish. *Courtesy of Erik Son*

Opposite: Mark using one of the most utilized machines in the shop. *Courtesy of Andy White*

The first titanium bike we made, enjoying the sun at the Enve builder roundup. *Courtesy of John Watson, The Radavist*

One of our lightest builds, a rim brake Speciale with Super Record and Enve tubs coming in at 6.7 kg. *Courtesy of Erik Son*

PROVA
super record

Example of our gravel bike, the Mostro.
Courtesy of Erik Son

Titanium bottom bracket cluster.
Courtesy of Dave Rome

Pinion-gearbox-equipped MTB with Prova-designed sliding dropouts.
Courtesy of Josh Weinberg, The Radavist

Head tube detail on the Integrale.
Courtesy of Mason Hender

QUIRK CYCLES

LONDON, UK

Quirk Cycles was founded in London back in 2015, with the aim of making modern steel bikes for cyclists who didn't fit the mold of pro cyclist wannabes. As Rob points out, "The majority of cycling marketing, at the time, was geared towards selling *us* what the *pros* use, but myself, like many, didn't fit this pattern." Around this time, a number of riders started questioning the norms expounded by the industry. Some of those questions included the following: Were 23 mm tires really the ideal width? Is that race geometry road bike good for all-day riding? What frame material is best for my needs?

Rob explains that "two 'scenes' had started to emerge that would change the face of cycling forever—Ultra-Racing and Gravel Cycling." For the first time in his living memory, the market started to be led and informed by grassroots cycling cultures: "Cycle sales once dominated by skinny-tire road bikes changed to a sudden huge demand for bikes that were designed to be ridden for days on end over a multitude of surfaces." According to Rob, the only remotely suitable things the big companies could offer were CX frames. In his opinion, these all fell short of the demands of these new types of riders, so those riders turned to custom builders like himself.

Rob reconnected with bikes in the promise of adventure of ultra-racing and gravel, so he began designing bikes suited to these events: "To test out my bicycle design ideas, I signed up to ultra-events, where I would design, build, and race what I believed to be the ideal bike for the job." Rob says that

Pro Bikegear–commissioned Durmitor Race. Painted in Pro's signature blue with a marbled and real gold-leaf finish.
Courtesy of Nikoo Hamzavi Photographer

his designs became the basis for the models he sells today, taking their names from key locations in the race they took part in. For example, "the Durmitor is named after Durmitor National Park in Montenegro, from the 2016 edition of the Transcontinental. Likewise, the Kegety gained its moniker from a brutal 3,900-meter climb that inducted riders into the inaugural Silk Road Mountain Race. You get the idea." It was in these grassroots cultures that Rob found his start as a builder and his niche as a cyclist.

"Quirk Cycles has always been the sole work and output of myself, and throughout its nine years of existence, everything you see has passed through my hands," says Rob. He is the designer, manufacturer, consultant, and brand consultant. His workspace is therefore designed for efficiency and minimal tools: "Often you will see many frame builders' spaces full of heavy machinery like mills and lathes, but I worked hard to develop a construction process that needed minimal tooling. This is thanks to the use of additive manufacturing that allows me to 3-D-print key parts of the frame in stainless steel or titanium, dramatically increasing the efficiency of a build."

For Rob, there are so many aspects to building custom bikes to get excited about: "Designing the finish is always one that resonates with me, but also the deep satisfaction that comes after the moment I finish welding, seeing the progress and the realization of months of design and development in an instant." He's always loved the brazing process due to the primal draw of the flame, and the connection he feels to a process that has been performed in one form or another for thousands of years. He says, "There's something alchemic watching silver be drawn around steel through capillary action, and the fumes and smoke would have you believe Mephistopheles has been summoned." Parallel to this tradition, Rob is equally drawn to the modern processes of selective laser melting and cold metal fusion, which are used to create the metal 3-D parts used in his frames.

Inspiration for Rob's frames comes in many forms, such as cycling events, processes, and art: "Long-distance events give you a lot of time to think! Many of the design ideas of geometry and frame design are directly inspired by these events. Other models have been inspired by the processes I use. The Durmitor ULTRA and TITAN both have come about through a development of the 3-D printing process and the ability to be able to make steel and titanium bikes in ways that were not previously possible." For paint finishes, Rob gains inspiration from anything—a place of significance to a work of art. For example, the starting point for one of his favorite builds was just a color and a place—aubergine and Japan: "We ended with one of the most beautiful kintsugi-inspired finishes done to date."

Pro Bikegear–commissioned Durmitor Race. Painted in Pro's signature blue with a marbled and real gold-leaf finish. *Courtesy of Nikoo Hamzavi Photographer*

Although he often finds inspiration in far-off places, Rob recognizes that being based in London has been instrumental to what he does, and he counts himself lucky to be embraced and supported by that cycling community. Likewise, support and words of encouragement during an ultra-racing event left an indelible mark on Rob. As he points out, one of the most enjoyable aspects of ultra-racing is the psychological obstacles it presents, and part of the challenge is navigating these: "One of the biggest hurdles I think a lot of racers

Frame builder Rob Quirk checking tubes for roundness on his surface plate. *Courtesy of Nikoo Hamzavi Photographer*

encounter, especially in off-road races, is the 'getting off your bike and pushing' scenario. For many, to do this is tantamount to failure, and for me as well." This perception changed for Rob on a dusty road in Morocco: "I met a racer during the Atlas Mountain Race while pushing my bike, feeling dejected. We exchanged words, and he said something that has forever stayed with me:

> Walking is a tool; it's another weapon in your arsenal. When you can't ride, get off and push. Save your energy, stretch it out; you'll be the better for it. It was a revelation! Soon I found myself looking forward to the hike-a-bike sections; they offered a change, some respite, and, just like that, it was no longer defeat; suddenly it was progress! For the first time during a race, I saw walking as a benefit. This moment forever changed how I ride.

Frame builder Rob Quirk in his East London workshop. *Courtesy of Nikoo Hamzavi Photographer*

Emanuele's Durmitor ULTRA. Detail of the 3-D-printed seat cluster painted with terrazzo islands in candy paint by Jack Kingston. *Courtesy of Nikoo Hamzavi Photographer*

Emanuele's Durmitor ULTRA. Stainless-steel road bike with 3-D-printed head tube, cluster, and dropouts and custom paint by Jack Kingston. *Courtesy of Nikoo Hamzavi Photographer*

Vittoria CORSA

Lawrence's Kintsugi Mamtor. Kintsugi-inspired all-road bike pictured in Japanese garden. *Courtesy of Nikoo Hamzavi Photographer*

Lawrence's Kintsugi Mamtor. Detail of hand-painted finish of Kintsugi-inspired all-road bike painted by Velofique. *Courtesy of Nikoo Hamzavi Photographer*

Quirk SUPRACHUB. 29er drop-bar gravel bike in a translucent candy–raw rose-gold finish. *Courtesy of Nikoo Hamzavi Photographer*

Quirk SUPRACHUB. 29er drop-bar gravel bike in a translucent candy–raw rose-gold finish, detail of front end. *Courtesy of Nikoo Hamzavi Photographer*

RICHARD SACHS CYCLES

DEEP RIVER, CONNECTICUT, US

"I didn't want to be a bicycle maker; I became one," says Richard Sachs. Richard has been a bicycle maker, under his own name, since 1975. He holds strong opinions, is insightful, and shares many interesting anecdotes into the whys and wherefores of his trade, as he likes to call it.

Writing skills, a competition, an overbooked college class, and a newspaper advertisement set Richard Sachs on the path to becoming a bicycle maker. Though Richard claims as a teenager he was a mediocre student, his writing skills were noticed and further encouraged by a teacher at the Peddie School. During his sophomore year, he entered a several-thousand-word short story in the schoolwide creative-writing contest and won. "Immediately, the affirmation was intoxicating, and I continued vigorously with pen and paper. By senior year, I saw myself as a writer," says Richard. He was accepted at Goddard College, and plans for a traditional September entrance were put in place. Over the summer, Goddard wrote to inform him that the class was overbooked, and suggested he wait until April to begin campus life.

While stocking shelves for a cosmetics company in the Empire State Building basement, Richard saw an advertisement in the *Village Voice* for a bicycle mechanic in northern Vermont. Richard says, "Though I had a bicycle at the time, I wasn't a rider, or a bike geek, and had no real knowledge that people raced them." Regardless, he took a one-way Greyhound bus to Vermont: "The next day I walked into the Ski Rack, classified ad in hand, and declared myself present for the job. They laughed. The position was already filled. Worse yet, in asking me about my experiences, I was told mine were less than sufficient anyway. This left me deflated."

Some people think of forks as aftermarket components, each with their own SKU. I believe otherwise and choose to make one for every frame that leaves my studio. *Courtesy of Brian Vernor*

With options quickly fading, he needed to find a way to redeem himself before starting at Goddard in April. He admits that he doesn't know where the thought came from, but he decided to write to several bicycle-making companies in England, offering himself up in return for allowing him to see what they do: "I'd convinced myself that being in a place where bicycles were made was cooler than being in a shop fixing them. I wanted to get even with the Ski Rack people for not hiring me."

One letter from Witcomb Lightweight Cycles in Deptford, a second-generation family business, came back in the positive. They agreed to let him come over and be a quiet observer. "Without missing a beat, I left Burlington, flew to Heathrow Airport, and within a week was going to work daily at the Witcomb shop," Richard says. During his stay in England, the Witcomb family was entering into a business relationship with Ed Allen from Connecticut, who was expanding his business, Sports East Incorporated, into the bicycle market. Nearing the end of Richard's stay, Barry Witcomb suggested he organize an interview with Witcomb USA, and he was offered a job. He says, "By now, my interest in writing and attending Goddard were waning. I was immersed in my new adventure and only nineteen years old. Thoughts of the unplanned life as a tradesman were soon replacing anything that previously involved using my imagination along with some writing implements."

About a year into his new life at Witcomb USA, Ed's relationship with his English partners was failing: "To shore up the business and to get frames to retailers who were waiting patiently for orders that were late, or never filled at all from London, Ed had the idea to make frames in Connecticut." Richard and Peter Weigle were the two people on staff tasked with this project. "With the experience of living and working next to real, live frame builders in London for almost a year, Peter and I, using Ed's blank checks and local resources, somehow created a small manufacturing business and began churning out frames," recalls Richard. While everyone was happy with the output, Richard admits that his adventure was becoming tedious, predictable, and routine, so he decided to leave.

By 1975, Richard decided to sublet the corner of a barn that a pal was renting: "My shop space and brand began that summer." Richard admits he felt confident enough with his abilities to fill orders, but lingering questions about the deferred writing course remained: "Years became decades. And despite all the time passing, I never took the initiative to roll back into my previous life as a student. On the other hand, I was never fully sure I knew what I was doing at the workbench. But people from all over the world were ordering my frames, and the following I had was my affirmation. Ultimately, I became a frame builder. But I never walked into a room wanting to be a frame builder, or assuming I could be a frame builder, or even thinking I was a frame builder."

For Richard, "Frame building is a creative process. One that can be tied to production methods, quotas, and price points," noting that it's a lot easier to reconcile the business side of things now than when his life was one big learning curve. He says he fought long and hard the notion that machines and staffs of people manning workstations could make bicycle frames the way frame builders made them: "I wanted so much to believe that the artisans and brands that I held in high regard, those who I considered muses and had pioneer status—I wanted to believe that their work was above reproach. We all need a special lens through which to view things on our way up; something must be the carrot, and someone must provide the inspiration." At the beginning of his career, he had role models too. But more than these, he says, "I believed that bicycle frames made *this way* were the Fabergé eggs, or the best from the best luthiers in Cremona, or the haute-est of haute couture all rolled into one. It wasn't so much about an individual making a bicycle that was the center of my fantasy as much as it was the fantasy itself. It included a world in which men who did this kind of work answered to a higher calling."

The line forms to the right and extends around the corner and down the block. *Courtesy of Richard Sachs*

For as long as Richard can remember, bicycle racing has reminded him of boxing because it's old school and rooted in the working class. He proffers this assessment of bicycle racing: "My sport is a prewar, premotorsports sport, and a pretelevised sport ordeal at its core. It's governed by retired racers who manage the teams and drive the cars that follow the events. These people, mostly older men, keep things in a state of arrested development. I follow it with all its foibles and transgressions and try to enjoy it as entertainment, nonetheless. It's a chore." Though, as he acknowledges, "my trade is part of this puzzle."

In his impressionable years, he considered frame builders to be the cornermen for those inside the rings—Coaches. Cutmen. Handlers. The guys who told the fighters what to do and what not to do: "In my mind—and this is a construct few will likely share—the men who design and make the bicycles each had their own followings, racers who'd depend on them to supply machines that could lead them to the finish line

A small selection of reinforcing pieces for my front fork assemblies.
Courtesy of Brian Vernor

ahead of all others." He explains, "There's no disputing that a relationship, a trust, existed between the frame builder and the athlete. I don't remember ever NOT wanting to be a part of this construct, be it real or simply the fantasy that keeps me looking forward. To make a better bicycle so that those in whose corners I sit will have the best tool for the job—this is the reason I come to the workbench each day."

As a lone builder, Richard has operated from six different workspaces over the years; the first three as a renter, and the others as a homeowner with an adjacent studio: "By the third space, which came in the early '90s, I began paying more attention to the atmosphere of my environment rather than the actual work performed within it." He transitioned the interiors from simply a room with benches and tools into what he envisioned as a gallery: "Even when I fell short of expectations, the driver always was to have a clean and elegant studio in which frames were made, rather than it being a production shop. It hasn't always been easy to meet this standard, but it's still the one I adhere to." His current studio is a two-story building, steps away from his back porch. The first floor is where the work is carried out, and the upstairs is filled with shelving on which many years of his personal ephemera and current inventory are neatly stored. Richard says, "I keep nothing on any walls to remind myself, or anyone who enters my front door, who I am or what I've done for fifty-plus years. No articles. No posters. No mementos. No race trophies. Nothing." Richard says there's a balancing act of chaos when he stands at the bench to make a bicycle frame. The part he loves the most is the part at the very beginning: "Nothing after this is better." Just like a writer with pen paused over a blank sheet of paper, he is about to make his mark! Richard puts it this way:

> When the pipes are mitered and I'm satisfied all the elements meet a standard, that's when the torch is lit for the first time. Little pieces of metal balancing on round tubes. Each has a function and an exact place to be. The tactile senses are heightened when the smell of an oxyacetylene flame dances on a pile of surrendering paste flux. But when the business end of the brazing rod I'm holding begins its travel under and ever so slightly around every joint, that's when I become overloaded by the scent of heat and the mastery necessary to shepherd molten filler into places;

I command it to go. Bicycle making as—A conversation. A collaboration. A path. Training and experience be damned. It's the same for good design and workmanship. These are only parts of the equation. There are also the materials, as well as the tools I hold. Making is also a compromise between the ideal you hold and the parts you use. Everyone speaks. My role is to tame the beast, that stuff on my bench. There are the days when the metal tells you what it wants to be. And all you can do is take the ride. But the material does talk to you. And you must listen. For fifty-plus years I've listened. The conversation will continue. Someday, the material may hear me too.

Richard says, "Frame builders are obsessed with being as precise as possible. How straight is it? How long is it? A strange lot, us. But when it comes to metrology, few things separate the wheat from the chaff like an exact measurement." Starting in London, in what Richard describes as a typical Dickensian shop with the barest of basics, it was imperative that he find a way to "hone his intuition, senses, muscle memory, and all traits that help a man make something better when there's no way to check. I've found that if you ask ten frame builders about the accuracy of their work, you'll get twelve answers, and two of them will need a mediator to determine what on earth they were saying." Richard refers to the Florentine tailor Antonio Liverano, who wrote, "There's the centimeter, the millimeter, and then the human eye." Richard states, "In my trade, speaking in the abstract is an art form as well as a defense mechanism. That's why I say, '*You can't measure what you don't see.*' And I often add, 'At Richard Sachs Cycles, I am the precision tool.'"

Antonio Colombo (*left*) invited me to Milan, where I was the guest speaker at Columbus's centennial celebration, held at his art gallery. *Courtesy of Brian Vernor*

Richard's design influences and inspiration are drawn from a range of disciplines: "In no particular order, Jimmy D'Aquisto (luthier), Paul Laubin (oboe maker), Eva Zeisel (ceramicist and industrial designer), George Nakashima (woodworker), Anthony Mangieri (pizzaiolo), Jiro Ono (chef), Philippe Dufour (watchmaker), and my wife—the lovely Deb, are among those who most inspire me."

Like many bike builders, Richard receives many letters from clients expressing gratitude for their newly delivered Richard Sachs bicycles: "One that has always stood out is the following typewritten letter":

Dear Mr. Sachs:

Late this summer I ordered and now have taken delivery of a bicycle frame made by you. What a wonderful thing! It actually makes me feel young again. Very few things I have ever owned have given me as much pleasure as your frame and that bicycle. It is particularly beautiful to look at. The details on the frame are outstanding. Even more important to me, it makes me feel young again. It is the smoothest, most perfectly balanced bicycle I could ever imagine having. If the truth be known, it has become a major distraction from the work I should be doing at the Art Museum, and there are moments when I think it should be on exhibit here and not encumbered by my body going through the Pennsylvania countryside. However, its role is the latter, and it is doing it perfectly. I can never imagine having a bicycle that I couldn't think of improving in some ways. Now I have a bicycle which I could not imagining improving. I am only surprised at all the wonderful things it and I can do together.

The letter was signed:

"Robert Montgomery Scott
President
Philadelphia Museum of Art"

Richard acknowledges that it took years—decades, really, for him to be comfortable landing where the winds blew him. So, what else is Richard doing with his life when not making bicycles?—"Living it."

An RSCX rider *at speed* during the Rochester Cyclocross UCI C1 event. *Courtesy of Brian Vernor*

These are 3-D-printed versions of my B.I.F.I.™ rear dropouts. All my cast parts are sampled before I sign off on final production. *Courtesy of Brian Vernor*

A world outside your window isn't free.
—Tanita Tikaram. *Courtesy of Brian Vernor*

A mountain of *Richie-Issimo™* bottom bracket shells to remind us of Devils Tower. *Courtesy of Richard Sachs*

Because there's nothing more beautiful than the way the ocean refuses to stop kissing the shoreline, no matter how many times it's sent away. —Sarah Kay. *Courtesy of Richard Sachs*

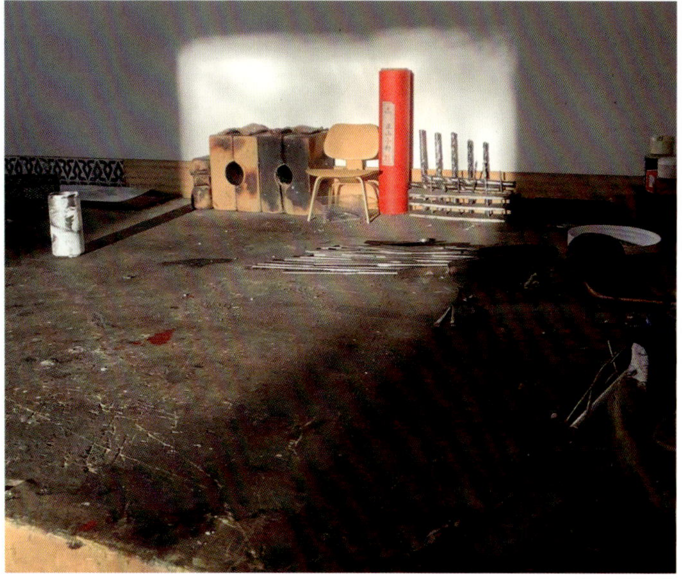

I'm not here to create disorder; I'm here to arrange disorder. *Courtesy of Richard Sachs*

RIZZO
CYCLES
#RIDEHARD
UFO
DRIP
SENTINEL

RIZZO CYCLES

MADRID, SPAIN

"Bicycles mean good vibes worldwide," according to Rizzo Cycles owner Rubén Durán. During his childhood, bikes filled his summers with joy. He then reconnected with them as an adult in a more tangible way: "I could have chosen something like guitar building or another quirky endeavor, but bikes were an integral part of my daily life during a pivotal moment, so they felt like the right choice." Rubén later discovered that his great-grandfather was a blacksmith, which makes him wonder if there was some blood connection to them both working with steel.

Rizzo grew from Rubén's need for a backup plan while working as a sound engineer. He says, "With numerous free days each month, I was searching for a way to fill the gaps between jobs, so I started exploring the idea of making bikes." During the COVID-19 pandemic, everything took a different turn, and his hobby became his profession. Rubén runs a one-man operation from what he describes as a compact, cluttered 30-square-meter workshop, filled with aged, heavy machinery, handling everything except the painting: "I started with just a handful of hand files. Over time, I crafted tools to aid in the process (some of which I still use) and made significant financial investments to gradually acquire bigger equipment." His machinery includes a lathe and two milling machines, totaling over 2 tons of steel. He even converted one of the milling machines into a sander, which served as his go-to machine for a long time. Rubén also has a deep

Rizzo TIG-welding a frame. *Courtesy of Rocío María Morales Alvarez*

affection for his machines: "Despite their age, they operate flawlessly. In fact, it's something that continues to amaze me every day; my lathe is around sixty years old!"

When a bike is commissioned, Rubén engages with customers from the very beginning and guides them through the entire process. He says, "It can be exhausting, but this is the model [that] customers seek. They want me to be involved in every step, from designing and cutting to welding and finishing their bikes." Rubén's favorite part of the process is welding the frame, tacking it, and removing it from the jig: "That moment when tubes transform into a frame." It is thrilling to create functional, tangible objects, fulfilling the dreams of customers, and crafting things entirely by hand: "I start my week with a few tubes and end it with a complete bicycle frame that didn't exist before."

Rubén's primary design influences come from Italian masters such as Pegoretti, Zullo, and Legor: "Their use of fat tubes and unique dropout designs and the pursuit of performance without sacrificing the overall aesthetics of the bike are inspiring." Rubén aims for minimalist frames with exceptional paintwork and has strived, over the years, to stay rooted in the ethos of creating without unnecessary complications: "Currently, I'm venturing into titanium and modern techniques, such as 3-D-printed parts. I don't want to remain static; I see this journey as a continuous learning process with no definite end." Having an active mind and the ability to think outside the box is crucial. With such a demanding job, he believes you have to earn your position through your hard work and dedication.

Every time he receives a message from one of his customers, it feels like a gift: "They travel with their bikes or use them for daily workouts, but from time to time, they remind me of the wonderful job I did and express their delight. It's heartwarming." Rubén recalls one customer saying, "You have to tell me how it feels to work making people happy." He once built a bike for a skeptical friend who didn't believe in the benefits of steel. He designed a bike for him to test, and the plan was to then sell it in his shop. Rubén says, "After his first ride, he texted me to express his amazement with the ride quality. It has become the bike he rides the most since then."

There isn't much time outside the workshop for Rubén, but when there is, most of his free time is spent with his partner. He is also trying to revive old hobbies, such as playing the guitar. Rubén says, "Surprisingly, I have to make an effort to go out and ride my own bikes. It can be challenging to find the motivation to pedal when you're surrounded by bike-related work all day: I have put literally everything into this for the past seven years, and it is now I have started to find balance." Rubén's focus is on what lies ahead for his brand and what he aims to achieve. "Currently, I'm venturing into Titanium and modern techniques, such as 3-D-printed parts, which will evolve considerably overtime. I don't want to remain static; I see this journey as a continuous learning process with no definite end." Five years from now, he envisions settling in the countryside, far from the bustling city, with a cozy backyard workshop and a few farm animals: "I want to be in a place where I can step out the back door and ride on the trails. That's the direction I want my brand to take. I can hardly believe what I've accomplished. Just like in cycling, I keep moving forward to avoid falling."

Rubén in his workshop with his main tool, the frame jig.
Courtesy of Rocío María Morales Alvarez

Opposite: Synth Wave vibes on this 29er ADVenture gravel.
Courtesy of Nil Camarasa, the Service Course

(Almost) all this by hand. *Courtesy of Gianfranco Tripodo*

Rizzo means "curl," and it´s obvious why I choose it as my brand name. *Courtesy of Gianfranco Tripodo*

I brought this Pedrazzoli from Italy on my van and modified it by myself. As far as I know, there are only five more machines like this, only owned by Italian frame builders. *Courtesy of Gianfranco Tripodo*

The steel stallion that opened the eyes of my skeptical friend. *Courtesy of Victor Merino, Sanferbike*

Maria enjoying Gorafe desert sunset.
Courtesy of @ athleticaffair

A timeless classic, a 2023 rim brake road bike.
Courtesy of Enve Composites

KING

Titanium gravel, fully integrated. *Courtesy of @huffy808foto/@dylanvanweelden*

All paint jobs are as custom as the frames, perfectly executed by Muse Bikes. *Courtesy of Ale Cubino*

When I built this full-suspension, I felt I could build anything. *Courtesy of Enve Composites*

HUNT
P ZERO
P ZERO
Aerodynamicist

SCARAB CYCLES

ANTIOQUIA, COLOMBIA

Scarab Cycles was established in 2018 with the dream of creating a custom-made bicycle that would resemble Colombian cycling culture. "Bikes are embedded in our DNA in Colombia," says Scarab Cycles founder, Santiago Toro: "We come from a nation where bikes, bike racing, bike commuting, and everything about bikes simply happen in a natural way." Building custom-made bikes enables Scarab to engage in conversations with customers on how they ride, and offers them a more enhanced experience with a product that meets their very specific riding requirements.

Santiago describes Colombia as a tough and challenging country, where high-performing bikes are needed to handle long climbs, steep and twisty downhills, and rough roads: "Colombian culture is loud, cheerful, and rooted to nature. We wanted our bikes to reflect that, no matter on which place on Earth, it should be an homage to Colombia."

Once established, Scarab comprised a five-person team with one big thing in mind: to "create everything in-house with the highest standards possible," explains Santiago. Now they are a twelve-person team working in a shop located in El Retiro, a beautiful mountain town on the outskirts of Medellín. Here they split their time among production, procurement, accounting, sales, design, logistics, and customer service. "Doing the cutting, welding, and paint finishing under

Santa Rosa Integrated road bike painted with the Magdalena paint scheme. *Courtesy of MADE Bike Show, @huffy808foto and @dylanvanweelden*

the same roof ensures the highest quality on every bike and allows us to work with a lot of flexibility in terms of design," says Santiago.

For the Scarab team, the most exciting thing about building a bike is being able to share a whole new perspective with a rider who most likely didn't know their ride could be taken to a new level. It's making a dream come true. As Santiago puts it, "The funny thing is, most people didn't really know what that dream was when they started the process. People come to us looking for a beautiful bike, and they end up having an amazing-looking bike that they simply want to ride."

When designing a bike, the Scarab team has in mind an overarching concept they call "Telepathic Handling": "For us, it means that the bike so perfectly fits the expectations, riding style, and sensitivity of the rider that it has a connection that goes beyond known sensorial and physical interactions." Although acknowledging that this narrative may be an exaggeration, they do take their "Telepathic Handling" concept very seriously: "We design a bike that you will handle and guide without even noticing it. For us, a bike is not too tweaky or too sluggish in handling; it was simply built or selected for the wrong rider." The handling is important to Scarab for this reason: "What is the action you do the most on a bike? Nope . . . it is not pedaling. During a bike ride, all of the time, you are riding (handling) your bike."

From an aesthetic point of view, Scarab draws a lot of inspiration from Colombian culture, nature, and the cycling tradition of the mighty "Escarabajos," a term used for Colombian pro cyclists in the pro peloton: "Our country is full of unique things like a 'Chiva Bus' that enables us to create unique-looking bikes with an amazing story behind them." Dario Pegoretti is another big influence on their paintwork: "We spray every bike in a way that will show a particular aspect of our culture, natural abundance, or cycling tradition."

Since Chivas are a unique part of Colombian culture, Santiago tells a surprising story about the first order they received from Singapore:

> The customer wanted a "Chiva" painted bike. This was something we couldn't believe. There is nothing more Colombian than a Chiva Bus! And it was going to Singapore?! For us, this was amazing . . . it meant a lot to be able to send a little piece of Colombian culture there. It meant that what we did had meaning, more than what we could imagine.

When he's away from the Scarab workshop, Santiago enjoys the outdoors for biking, hiking, or fishing. He also has a love for radio-controlled cars and planes, which, he says, "sparked a lot of what I do today. From design to fine-tuning steering setups and understanding weight distribution."

A Santa Rosa Integrated road bike with the Campesina paint scheme. *Courtesy of Nicolás Muñoz*

Scarab Cycles frameset manufacturing module. *Courtesy of David Jaramillo, A-Burra entre Montañas*

Scarab Cycles Paramo painted with the Chiva theme. *Courtesy of Scarab Cycles*

Brake bridge getting hand-finished before brazing it to the frameset. *Courtesy of David Jaramillo, A-Burra entre Montañas*

Scarab Letras rim brake painted with the Colombian flag. *Courtesy of Scarab Cycles*

Paint process: unmasking the Hojas de Café paint scheme. *Courtesy of Scarab Cycles*

The Jungla displayed at the Enve Gordeo. *Courtesy of Enve Composites*

A Scarab Letras Rimbrake climbing las Palmas. *Courtesy of David Jaramillo, A-Burra entre Montañas*

Riding in the Colombian coffee lands. *Courtesy of Nicolás Muñoz*

SCHÖN STUDIO

SQUAMISH, BRITISH COLUMBIA, CANADA

Danielle Schön describes herself as an artist first who learned to become a fabricator. Thus, art informs most of her design choices. She says, "I grew up immersed in art—drawing, painting, crafting, sewing. As a teenager, I found creative outlet in photography and, ultimately, studied fine-art photography in college. Even while studying photography, I found that often my favorite part of the process was the lead-up to taking the photos—building and creating props and styling sets." Shortly after school, and a brief stint in the corporate world in an unrelated job, Danielle found her way into trade school to learn how to weld. Thereafter came machining, quality control, and nondestructive testing. Around the same time, Danielle was riding and racing bikes. She says, "I combined my interest in art and fabrication with my love for bicycles and initially learned how to build bike frames from both Paul Brodie and Koichi Yamaguchi." Building a few frames ignited a strong creative spark, and Danielle knew she had to pursue it as far as she could: "A decade later, here we are, and I'm still chasing that same spark, burning as bright as ever."

Danielle defines the bicycle as an interesting intersection of art and design, of form and function. "There is the opportunity to have a wild, almost endless sense of creativity and customization, but at the same time they require a very precise set of constraints to function properly," she says. Danielle finds bike building an extremely challenging yet fun space to play in because it pushes your creative boundaries while still ensuring a well-fitting, functional performance machine.

Danielle is a sole builder, who describes Schön Studio as not a company, or a brand, or a factory full of people. Her priority is feeding her creative desires, and, as an artist, it is hard to relinquish any of that control to someone else—even an assistant or a shop hand. She says, "Ultimately, my goal is to make something from my brain, with my hands, birth it to life into a beautiful or functional object, or, hopefully, both. I am what I call 'reluctantly branded.' I have to package myself to some extent to be able to make a living as an artist, with digital branding and enough details on paper in order to pay the bills. I lucked into the perfect surname for my craft and my business—*Schön* meaning 'beautiful' in German."

Danielle creates her bicycles in a medium-sized shop on her property. It is tucked under a 170-year-old oak tree, which often gives good perspective on life and on beauty. She says, "The shop provides enough space for the basics, a few larger-footprint specialty machines, a solid fabrication table, and being able to spread a project out over a few work surfaces until it all comes together." The space enables her to remain focused on the core of what she wants to achieve without a lot of extra fluff.

This stay placement is a visual and functional design choice, allowing internal routing to remain fully hidden the length of the frame. *Courtesy of Danielle Schön*

When creating a new bike, Danielle best sums up the process in the following passage she once wrote:

> Building something from nothing is fascinating. To pluck a passing thought from the sky and turn it into something tactile. To make feeling take shape or to mold the sense of adventure into metal.
>
> Hopes and dreams made real through blood, sweat, and tears. Made by hand—a piece of yourself in everything—the good, the bad, the ugly.
>
> The smell of oil and ore and the ability to create, in perpetuity, for life & death.
>
> What more could we ask for?

Taking ideas, dreams, wishes, and questions and translating them into a physical object is a combination of art, science, and technology: "Some might even say witchcraft—knowing just how much of each part is required, no more, no less. There is no true equation or defined process. Each object requires new and different considerations from the last. Every one is a question, an opportunity, an adventure, a riddle, a mountain to be summited, all at once."

During the process of making ideas, dreams, and wishes come to fruition, Danielle is particularly fond of lug fabrication and hand carving from scratch. "I think it offers the ultimate level of design control and opportunity to influence every line and intersection on a frame design. It is absolutely a labor of love and requires full immersion in the journey rather than glossing over the details to rush to the destination," she says.

Danielle's bicycles are influenced by classic, strong design that feels intentional and well considered as a complete object: "Nothing left out and nothing extra or unnecessary. Clean, bold, and curated." Equally, she likes the complete opposite, "art and designs that are completely exploratory, things that evoke raw feeling, something that offers many questions and no resolutions." These elements are often such a good starting point for her own curiosity and thoughts to jump off from and see where they take her. Danielle also looks to makers from all types of crafts that evoke this level of curation, seeing what can be learned, regardless of how different or similar our materials are. She says, "Inspiration can come from anywhere, and I strive to be present enough to see it wherever it is offered—fine art in all mediums, influences from builders I admire, shapes and sounds and experiences in nature, architecture in the city, and fleeting moments in the human condition."

Danielle Schön fillet brazing the front triangle of a bicycle frame in her Squamish, British Columbia, studio. *Courtesy of Pat Valade, The Radavist*

Danielle's location also influences the type of bikes she builds. "Living in the mountain bike capital of the country, most of my recent builds have been trail and adventure oriented. Regardless of where I'm living and what my local riding is like, I am always interested in building design-forward bicycles of any form or style," she says. It is particularly satisfying and something that always puts a smile on Danielle's face when a customer tells her that the bike she built for them is a dream bike that has quickly become their favorite: "I know functionally that my designs and fit are good, but hearing that confirmed by a glowing review of the first ride from a customer really never gets old."

If Danielle wasn't building bikes, she would still be doing something creative and hands on, a constant goal throughout her life. She says, "When I was young, I was into sewing and imagined a future in textile and costume design. In college that morphed into an interest in storytelling through photography and pursing my own studio or gallery space." The common thread has always been to have an outlet of creativity as the core to sustain her through life: "Currently it is metal fabrication and bicycle building—who knows if it will stay that way forever or what it may evolve into next. When I'm not building bikes, I'm likely riding them, eating good snacks, being cozy reading novels with my cuddly orange cat, spending time in nature, and contemplating life."

Cargo bikes offer a host of design opportunity with both fit and function in mind. *Courtesy of Josh Weinberg, The Radavist*

Subtle tube bends keep a consistent line through the length of the bike. Double top tubes provide segmented storage. *Courtesy of Josh Weinberg, The Radavist*

This track bike features lugs, dropouts, and other details made from Damascus steel, then Schön-forged and hand-carved herself. *Courtesy of Jarrod A Bunk*

The seat lug is hand-forged Damascus steel that was welded into a lug blank and then hand-carved into fine points for a classic look. *Courtesy of Jarrod A Bunk*

A modern mullet hard tail that has a fast, flowy feeling, a compliment to its lush surroundings. *Courtesy of Danielle Schön*

A mirror-polished stainless-steel badge offers both bold branding and a structural gusset for the hard-tail design. *Courtesy of Danielle Schön*

A hand-carved wraparound wing lug is a design feature on a sleek road bike.
Courtesy of Danielle Schön

The hard lines on this mini mountain bike evoke a brutalist design. *Courtesy of Josh Weinberg, The Radavist*

Loonies brazed to the fork crown are a nod to old-school BMX design. *Courtesy of Josh Weinberg, The Radavist*

SUEESS FRAMEWORKS

ZÜRICH, SWITZERLAND

Stefan Sueess states, "If you grew up in the Swiss countryside in the 1970s, the bicycle was probably the only way to explore beyond the village. Some had motorcycles or their moms drove them, but I had a racing bike as a boy and rode it up the hills that surrounded the village." Stefan's free time was all about tweaking his bike, putting on new tires, or adjusting the handlebars a bit lower: "The bike has been a part of my life and my little taste of freedom for as long as I can remember."

SUEESS Frameworks grew out of necessity, Stefan explains: "I'm a road bike enthusiast but discovered about ten years ago that mountain bikes could be a lot of fun too. Unfortunately, I couldn't find a bike I really liked, and I didn't want an aluminum frame. So, I thought, why not try building a hard-tail mountain bike myself? And that's where it started." Although not a daredevil on the trails, Stefan still has that bike and takes it out of the basement to explore the nearby hills, now and then. Stefan says, "That first bike planted the seed, and I wanted to dive deeper into the craft. Eventually, I felt the need to replace chance with skill and craftsmanship to produce even-higher-quality frames." That's when titanium entered Stefan's life, leading to a long period of hard work and lots of trial and error with this material. He says, "Today, I feel an incredible satisfaction as I glide through the woods on my self-built titanium gravel bike, and I can imagine what my customers feel."

Stefan is a one-man operation who crafts titanium frames in a small garage, building one bike at a time, according to the customer's requests and specific rider specifications. During each bike build, it's the welding that enthralls Stefan. "Nothing is as fascinating as watching metal melt and fuse back together. When everything fits, it's almost like a meditative process, where a bicycle frame is slowly created, point by point, from a few pieces of tubing. You can only truly understand this once you've experienced it yourself," he says.

He still gets a thrill thinking about his hands creating such a mechanically simple vehicle that represents freedom, joy, and adventure: "Unchanged for over a hundred years, it's the embodiment of efficient and peaceful mobility. Even if it can become a status symbol these days, a bicycle is still a device that can take you from point A to point B, and, if needed, beyond the horizon to explore uncharted territories. Quietly and simply, powered by your own muscles."

Commenting on his design influences and inspiration, Stefan says, "I got into craftsmanship through cycling, and design came through craftsmanship. Before I built my first frame, design wasn't a big concern because everything has been invented already. A bicycle is simply two frame triangles joined together. It's that simple; there's no need for fancy designs. So, most of my bikes have a traditional look based

Workshop at night. Exterior view into my workshop. My workshop is set up in a garage on the property of our house in Zürich. Handmade individual pieces made of titanium are created in a minimal amount of space. *Courtesy of Gae2tan Bally, Keystone*

on classic road bike geometries." Whether it's city or touring bikes, SUEESS bikes all carry that traditional bicycle appearance, with no extravagant or overly complicated designs. For Stefan, a bicycle frame always reflects the rich tradition of bike building, so he sticks with what feels familiar and proven: "In short, the design is guided by its intended purpose—form follows function." It might sound cliched, but in Stefan's opinion, it is the basis of any good bike geometry. He says, "Depending on the riding experience you want to have, you can use the head tube angle, the rake of the fork, or, for example, the length of the wheelbase to make the bike behave the way you want it to. Depending on the size of the frame triangles and the choice of tube diameters, you can determine how stiff or flexible a frame will feel. This will all vary from customer to customer and depend heavily on the rider's habits and desires."

A significant portion of Stefan's creative inspiration is drawn from the work of fellow craftsmen. Global trends also affect customer demands, such as the growing popularity of gravel biking. Stefan says, "In the contemporary interconnected world, the idea of finding inspiration purely from local sources has become increasingly rare." Instead, Stefan believes that the field has evolved into a global community of artisans and enthusiasts who continually exchange ideas, techniques, and design philosophies. This global exchange of knowledge has resulted in a convergence of ideas and practices, where builders from diverse corners of the world shape the future of frame design. Right now, the new possibilities of metal 3-D printing are opening up unimagined design and performance possibilities, especially for frame builders who produce individual, bespoked pieces.

Welding a head tube to the down tube on a titanium frame. Welding titanium is a very complex process that requires absolute precision and perfect preparation. During welding, no oxygen may come into contact with the weld seam. That's why the entire frame is covered with protective gas (argon) both from the inside and outside. Full concentration is required during this step. *Courtesy of Gae2tan Bally, Keystone*

Receiving complimentary, direct feedback on a bike build is always satisfying, particularly when it's from a friend, as Stefan retells in the following story:

> I once rode over the Passo dello Stelvio, the legendary pass of the Giro d'Italia, with a friend. He was on a steel bike I built years ago, and I was on my new titanium prototype. On the descent, he went really fast, and I followed him at a slower pace for a few minutes. Just before Bormio, he stopped, waited for me, and said, "You know, I trust my frame builder 100 percent." That's probably the best compliment I've ever received. It wasn't about a flashy paint job or fancy components; it was about the essence of cycling. Riding down the pass, wind in your hair, smoothly leaning into curves.

Before becoming a bike builder, Stefan identifies several turning points in his life: "After initially training as a primary-school teacher, I studied history and geography. I worked as a photojournalist for over a decade, founded a brewery from scratch, and even taught at a vocational school before I started building bicycle frames. Who knows, maybe the next turning point is just around the corner, and life will bring something entirely new my way. You're most focused when you venture into the unknown, and life is never more exciting than when you face new challenges every day."

Away from his workshop, Stefan takes time out to ride his bikes, soak in the scenery, and think about ways to improve his next build. That is, when he's not enjoying moments with his wife and two sons: "Sometimes, I tinker in the workshop, working with metal or wood or try to learn a CAD program, then realize it was easier to learn new things when I was younger. At a certain age, you might just have to go the extra mile to acquire new inspiration and skills. That's what makes being involved with bikes, craftsmanship and design so valuable."

The PBB1, cockpit. Fully integrated with Deda Gera carbon handlebar, Deda Superbox stem, and Deda Gera EDGE carbon fork. *Courtesy of SUEESS Frameworks*

The PBBL. Made for fast laps off the beaten track. Fast gravel bike with fully integrated cable routing. Dropouts and the seat tube–seat stay connection are made of 3-D-printed titanium. The bike clearly has racing genes. The geometry is based on road race bikes, with a slightly flatter head angle and a little more trail than a road racer. Thanks to the short wheelbase, it is very agile in handling and therefore a real fun machine for fast laps on forest paths and simple single-tracks. *Courtesy of SUEESS Frameworks*

The ride. Climbing Mount Uetliberg above Zürich.
Courtesy of SUEESS Frameworks

Bicycle in front of the rider . . . short break during a ride.
Courtesy of SUEESS Frameworks

SUEESS
Titanium
CUSTOM CRAFTED
WOLF TOOTH

Top tube–seat tube assembly on my Cobra frame-building jig. *Courtesy of Gae2tan Bally, Keystone*

Checking the bends of a self-bent chainstay on the printed plan. All seat stays and chainstays are bent by hand to the required dimensions and then checked for correctness on a plan. *Courtesy of Gae2tan Bally, Keystone*

Checking the alignment of the frame on the alignment table. Each frame is checked for alignment after the first welding pass and after it has been completely welded. *Courtesy of Gae2tan Bally, Keystone*

Opposite: The PBBL, head badge. Follow the wild boar . . . 3-D-printed stainless-steel head badge. *Courtesy of SUEESS Frameworks*

29er MTB. *Courtesy of John Watson*

SYCIP DESIGNS

SANTA ROSA, CALIFORNIA, US

"Everybody remembers when they first learned to ride a bike. It's fun!! And it's still fun riding now as an adult. It just brings you back to your childhood, and it's a great way to explore the outdoors and get exercise at the same time," says owner Jeremy Sycip. During his first year in art school, he worked part time at a bike shop, loved riding his mountain bike with friends, and occasionally joined in local MTB races. He then realized he wanted to learn how to build bike frames, so he did an apprenticeship with Rock Lobster and took a frame-building class with Albert Eisentraut at UBI (United Bicycle Institute). Learning how to build bike frames confirmed that Jeremy wanted to pursue bicycle building as a career.

Sycip Designs was established in 1992 by Jeremy and his older brother Jay. "We had a couple different shops in San Francisco, California, where we were building custom steel, aluminum, and titanium frames. We also offered TIG, fillet-brazed, and lugged frames," says Jeremy. Occasionally other companies contacted them to build frames. In 2001, they moved to Santa Rosa, California, and began painting their own bikes, expanded to five to six employees, and did everything in-house. Then, in 2008, they decided to sell the paint side of the business, and Jay moved to Oregon.

Jeremy now works by himself in a small workshop behind his house, where he does his customer fittings and builds custom-made steel, aluminum, and titanium frames. He says, "It's exciting fitting them to their frame and getting to hear what they are looking for in a bike, then making something from scratch that someone can actually ride." During the construction phase, Jeremy nominates his TIG welder as his favorite tool to use: "I love welding. I guess I like sticking metal together and making something useful and functional. And after thirty-plus years, it's still fun!"

Jeremy's location in Sonoma County has a bearing on the types of bikes his customers want him to build. As he points out, his house and workshop sit between two great parks, where mountain biking and road riding happen all year round. He says, "The roads are not super smooth, so I mostly build a lot of mountain bikes, larger-tire road bikes, and gravel bikes."

For design influences and inspiration, Jeremy likes making things that follow function: "My frames are pretty traditional looking. I just want to make sure the frames fit the rider and are built for their needs and purpose. I do attend some bicycle shows; check out trends in motorcycles, cars, and furniture; and get inspired that way. As Jeremy points out, there is a design feature on his frames that everyone asks about—the wishbone design on the seat stays that he caps with pennies or dimes. The story is this: "In the early '90s when V brakes came out for mountain bikes, they were really strong and flexing frames quite a bit. I wanted to make the frames stronger, so I started using 19 mm stays and came up with the wishbone design to stiffen it up. Then I realized a penny was the correct size for capping the tubes. Less than what a machine shop was quoting me to make caps. So, problem solved! Win-win!"

Jeremy also has another story, relayed to him by another person, about Robin Williams and a Sycip bike. He says,

> Robin Williams wanted to buy one of my bikes, one that was sitting in a shop window in San Francisco. He came early one morning to buy it, but the shop was still closed, and he ended up falling asleep in front of the shop. When the owner came to open up, noticing someone lying near the door, he gently nudged him and asked him to move somewhere else. When Robin woke up, he said he just wanted to buy the bike in the window. About a year after that happened, I finally met Robin, and he did confirm the story was true, and we had a good laugh. Such a funny guy, and he wanted to let me know he loved the bike. Such an honor for me to know he wanted and bought one of my bikes and for him to personally confirm the story.

When not building bikes, Jeremy loves riding bicycles, motorcycles, and scooters. He also spends time with his family going on road trips, camping, or on vacation.

Penny cap on wishbone seat stays. *Courtesy of John Watson*

Checking tube length and butting. *Courtesy of John Watson*

Jeremy TIG-welding front triangle. *Courtesy of John Watson*

Tacking frame in jig fixture. *Courtesy of John Watson*

Tandem ride with my wife. *Courtesy of Sycip Designs*

Tandem MTB race with Miles. *Courtesy of Chris Wells*

Single-speed mountain bike. *Courtesy of Sycip Designs*

Head badge detail, close-up. *Courtesy of Erik Fenner, Chris King Components*

Sycip Gravel Bike. *Courtesy of Sycip Designs*

TJ CYCLES
FLYING GATE
STRONGLIGHT
RR511
DT SWISS
RESTRAP
handmade in germany

TJ CYCLES

KNIGHTON, POWYS, UK

Chris Yeomans was a kid in London during the '60s. He says, "I started cycling and biking to school with my friend, and we'd push ourselves to go that little bit faster each day. We rode all year round: sun, rain, and black ice; we didn't care. Anything but going by car or bus." After leaving home to attend agricultural college, Chris went into farming for about twelve years until it became apparent that you could go only so far without owning your own farm. So, Chris decided to train as a blacksmith and returned to college: "Turns out I was quite good at blacksmithing, and during the next twenty-eight years I was involved with some fascinating projects. I worked almost exclusively on my own, with much of the work done by hand, something that in the end was my undoing. After twenty-seven years, my body started falling apart. I knew it was time to find something else to do, which is when a seed that I had planted years previously started to grow."

Riding bikes was a big part of Chris's family life. When his kids started racing, he noticed that people were making handmade steel mountain bikes: "Steel frames that were light, rode well, and looked great." It wasn't until he read an article in *Dirt Magazine* about Ed Haythornthwaite's steel frames that he first thought, "I would like to do that." A seed that lay dormant in his mind for over ten years motivated him to mention to his family that he was thinking of doing a frame-building course. He says he received a unanimous "Go for it, Dad! So, that's exactly what I did in 2016 at the Bicycle Academy in Frome. I came home with my first frame well and truly hooked, already planning the next one."

Marcel's single-speed Gate setup in touring mode.
Courtesy of Marcel Le Bachelet, www.mkjlb.co.uk

The idea was to phase out the blacksmithing as the frame building increased. In the end, Chris thought, "It's now or never," so out went the anvil and in came the frame jig. "I already had many of the tools I needed in my workshop, so with the addition of the frame jig I was up and running," says Chris. Friends and friends of friends started hearing about the enduro frame he had built, and orders started to come in: "It was wonderful; all I had to do was quit the blacksmithing, which had been part of my life for so long," though he found it difficult to say no to people he had done work for who had also become good friends. In the end, he sold all the blacksmithing equipment he didn't need for frame building, and the family moved house and workshop. Chris says, "And then I met Trevor Jarvis."

Trevor in his workshop at Tenbury Wells, where many of his frames were created. *Courtesy of Jim Holland, Instagram@j.h.o.l.l.a.n.d.*

Trevor Jarvis had been building the Flying Gate bike since 1979; it was a design originally devised in 1935 by the Baines brothers, called the VS37 because of its short 37¾ inch (959 mm) wheelbase." As it turned out, Trevor, age eighty-six, was looking for someone to continue building the frame that had been so much a part of his life. To appreciate the development of the Flying Gate, Chris Yeomans encapsulates the history of the Baines brothers, which extends back before 1900, when Bill and Reg Baines's father had a cycle shop:

> Reg Baines joined his father in the shop in 1919 at the age of fourteen, but even before that, he had to assist in the workshop each evening after school from 5:00 to 7:00 p.m. and again on Saturday mornings. At that young age, he learnt to braze and stove enamel with the best of them. After a few years, Bill and Reg formed the W & R Baines Company, believed to have been founded around 1928. The company had been building standard frames, but in 1934 Reg designed and built the first vertical tube frame to achieve a shorter wheelbase and make a more responsive frame. The thoughts on this came about after a visit to watch a track meeting on a boarded track near Middlesbrough, UK. On the way home, Bill and Reg were discussing the stress and whip they had noted on the rear of the bikes, and they concluded that shorter chainstays would be an advantage.

Reg set about building a mockup frame less the seat tube, with the chainstays as short as possible. This was the birth of the first V38, a naked-looking frame with the seat pillar passing though the seat lug. Further thought was given to the design, and a short seat tube with twin struts was added. This was called the VS37. All testing of the VS37 was done on local hill climbs, with great success. They had achieved the responsiveness that Bill and Reg had been looking for, and the VS37 became known as the International TT. Full-scale manufacture didn't commence until 1936, when the new factory was built in Idle Road, Bradford. The frame proved to be ahead of its time, and with the success that riders such as Jack Fancourt and Jack Holmes were having at Brooklands, Donnington, and the Isle of Man, the design spoke for itself. The frame was selected for the Olympics, which was canceled due to the Second World War. After the war, production carried on until 1954, and, shortly after, the factory closed around 1958.

Skip to 1979, and Trevor Jarvis set up TJ Cycles in Burton-on-Trent. Trevor had ridden a VS37 he'd been asked to renovate, and he was impressed. He tracked down Bill Baines and got his approval to relaunch the bike and reregister the design under the name Flying Gate, which was an old nickname for the bike—a reference to the quirky square angles and quick-ride feel. In 1984, he moved to Tenbury Wells, where he continued to build frames until 2015, having dedicated over thirty-five years to this wonderful piece of British

Rear dropout on Marcel's Dovedale single-speed. *Courtesy of Marcel Le Bachelet, www.mkjlb.co.uk*

cycling history. During this time, Trevor built over six hundred Flying Gate frames, many of them with highly ornate hand-cut lugs. In the later years, Jeremy Cartwright and Liz Colebrook built frames under Trevor's guidance as he tried to find someone to carry on the design.

Chris says, "The tipping point for me was when we went along to the Flying Gate Weekend." It's an annual meeting of Flying Gate enthusiasts that attracts over fifty riders for a weekend of riding and lots of food. Ages range from seventeen to eighty-seven for the riders, with frames dating from the 1940s to the day before the weekend. Chris was blown away by the enthusiasm they had for the bike and their sense of community. Trevor talked about his need to find someone to take over the business, and Chris realized that it was an opportunity that, if overlooked, he could well regret for a long time: "So, in 2021 I took over the ownership of TJ Cycles but continue to liaise with Trevor on all things Flying Gate. Trevor finally handed his gas bottles back and officially retired at eighty-eight. We'll wait and see."

The business came with the frame jig that Trevor had built in the '70s: "Moving it out of his workshop for the first time in 40 odd years was a big step for someone who has dedicated so much of his life to building this frame." The jig takes pride of place in Chris's workshop, located behind his house, and is up there as one of his favourite pieces of equipment. Chris says, "It's a basic homemade item, but it is accurate. It has enough length to build a tandem, and, best of all, you can spin the frame through a full 360 degrees, making the process of brazing the frame so much easier. Not only is brazing a great way to build a frame, but I think it looks good too. I do some TIG welding, but I much prefer a brazed lug or fillet joint."

For Chris, the most exciting thing about bike building is the reaction he gets from people when they receive their new bike: "Not just on the day, but in the months ahead when they ride it, and it becomes part of their lives." He gets messages and photos from people telling him where they have been on the bike, and the reactions they get from people they meet. When someone tells Chris years after he made something for them how much they are still enjoying it, he knows he has done something worthwhile. These reactions and comments act as food for his soul. Chris says, "On one occasion, a guy called Dom had built up his bike and took it out for a shakedown ride around one of his local routes. When he got back, he checked his Strava and found he had eighteen new personal records. Later that week, he messaged me again, saying, 'I've been out on another circuit. I do a lot, and without really trying to go faster. I did a new personal best; incredible—I can hardly keep up with the bike.' That made me smile, but also, it's good to know the frames I am building are a bit special." Chris also loves that he's making something that is good both for the environment and for people's mental health: "It never fails to amaze me how quickly my well-being is lifted as soon as I get on a bike."

Each miter is hand-filed to a perfect fit. *Courtesy of Sabina Kinghorn*

As Chris points out, cycling is for many people a large part of their lives. How they feel about the bike they have is the key aspect of this part of their life. When that bike is made to fit them, they will get more enjoyment out of it and spend less time wondering about how it could be better: "To that end, I build bikes for people to keep for a long time. Quite contrary to today's throwaway society. Yes, we all change what we do as we get older, and cycling is no different, but I try to find out what a customer really enjoys—not what they have been told they should enjoy by the marketing giants in the industry. If I can work that out, I can make them a bike they will jump on at every opportunity. Now, that excites me."

Chris's design influences and inspiration come when something catches his eye: "It can be anything, really, not just metalwork. The line or shape of an item, the color, or the way the design comes together as a whole. These are the things that make me want to try new ideas." He recognizes that he has a long-won appreciation of work crafted by hand, the way people can move an idea from inside them and translate it through the tools they hold. For example, "blacksmithing is way more than hitting hot metal. I never really thought about the hammer in my hand; I would think about the item I wanted to create and watch it take shape, adjusting it until I got it right, from my mind to the metal. It took a long time to get to that stage, though; some of my early work was pretty dodgy." Chris acknowledges that he's been making stuff with his hands for so long now that it is easy to forget that not everyone can do it: "When I remember to stop and think about it, I feel very grateful to have the skills I have acquired over the years."

Moving to Knighton a few years ago, during the COVID-19 lockdown, has also influenced the type of bikes Chris builds: "We took the opportunity to thoroughly explore the local area. The cycling around here is just wonderful. So long as you don't mind climbing and potholes, oh yeah, and sheep poo!" According to Chris, The Flying Gate and hills are a must. "Personally, I am happy with a single ring up front, whether it's on my mountain bike or Flying Gate. He likes the simplicity of fewer gears and once he's ridden up a Welsh hill, he's ok with not peddling flat out on the descent: "Sometimes you must remember to take time and enjoy the ride. Also, it's a lovely nod to the early bikes before front derailleurs. That's not to say you can't have a double chain ring on a Flying Gate." A while back he built a flat bar gravel

When he's not touring, it gets switched to city-ripper mode. *Courtesy of Rae Wilding, www.raewilding.com*

Trevor and I at the twenty-fifth annual Flying Gate weekend. He's still riding at eighty-nine. *Courtesy of Chris Yeomans*

bike that was perfect for riding locally. "The design took off and I have made a run of them, all slightly different to suit the rider. Those were all Smithy Frameworks builds, my other brand."

When not building bikes, Chris would like to say he spends time touring the country with his wife, Dawn, on their own bikes. "Sometimes that is actually the reality and hopefully we can be organised enough to make it happen more often." Being keen outdoor swimmers, they sometimes combine a ride with a dip in the sea or some hidden pool in the Welsh hills. Chris built a bike trailer a while back so if the surf is good they might take the body boards, if it's flat the trailer is big enough to carry a paddle board, and that goes in instead: "Makes for a pretty good day out especially when shared with friends and family."

One very happy customer. Frank with his Dovedale Deluxe Special. *Courtesy of Frank Valentin*

The iconic seat cluster on a Flying Gate. *Courtesy of Frank Valentin*

The Flying Gate fifth lug. Each one is hand-cut. *Courtesy of Chris Yeomans*

Opposite: Trevor hand-cut many different lug designs over the years. These are on his own bike. *Courtesy of Jim Holland, Instagram@j.h.o.l.l.a.n.d.*

JARVIS
LIGHTWEIGHT FRAME BUILDER
TENBURY WELLS
• WORC •
SHIMANO

Irio Tommasini returning, by bike, after a winning race in the countryside around Grosseto. *Courtesy of unknown*

TOMMASINI

GROSSETO, ITALY

The story behind the Tommasini brand, founded in Tuscany in 1957, began when the founder, Irio Tommasini, fell in love with cycling and bicycles. At a young age, Irio saw, for the first time, the Milano–Sanremo peloton crossing Varazze, while he was spending his summer holidays in Liguria. The racers, the speed, the colors, and the people yelling out loud to support their champions got under his skin so deeply that he wanted to be part of this enchanted world. "His love for cycling grew after that event and brought a young Irio into this world of dreams," says Barbara Tommasini.

Irio started working as a mechanic in a bicycle shop to earn money to pay for a bike that he could race. According to Barbara, "Irio could have been a good racer, but he was more interested in frame building and innovations in this field. He even upgraded his racing bike by adding braze-on supports that were not available in late '40s frames." He then moved to Milan and Turin, where, in 1948, he was the designated apprentice of the best frame builder of the era—Giuseppe Pelà. Guiseppe was producing frames for the most-important and most-famous racers of the time, including Eddy Merckx. Under Guiseppe's tutelage, "Irio learned exquisite frame building," says Barbara. The two original brand names that Irio's frames were marketed under were Thomas and Tommasini, which continues to this day. Sadly, Irio Tommasini passed away in October 2024.

In the 1970s, Tommasini started to introduce stylish paintwork for their frames—"the Retinato," an original fishnet paint job. Tommasini claims that "since the early '80s, that paint finish became the most copied design." Also, in late '80s: "We set up a joint venture with a US company working in the aerospace fields to originate the first titanium tube sets to build a titanium bicycle frame. This resulted in the 1989 introduction of the Tommasini Mach Ti, an exquisite mix of technology and beauty."

The Tommasini brand still looks to the future by paying attention to the new trends, but always with strong roots and attention to high quality and details. Barbara describes the Tommasini headquarters as having a small but superb team of very skilled frame builders and technicians who continue a tradition of innovation: "Building a bike here at Tommasini is not like putting something together. It is more like giving birth to a creature. Every frame is considered, designed, and handbuilt through the process of handling, working, and welding every part. Every frame is unique and created to offer the customer not just a bike, but a mate." At Tommasini they believe that "for a true frame builder, a frame well built with metals is something with a soul, not just a piece to be ridden."

What really inspires the Tommasini team is the feedback they receive from their customers. This is in the form of letters and visits from Tommasini bikes owners who regard their bikes as friends and riding partners, with which they share moments of their life. For example, they received a visit from a lady who had ridden her Tommasini bike across Europe, just to read them an amazing letter she had composed in Italian: "She wanted to be sure we understood deeply what the Tommasini bike meant for her—not a just a bike, but a true friend that helped her survive during the COVID-19 pandemic by giving her the motivation to live and enjoy life during those tough times."

Never averse to injecting a bit of a cheeky sense of humor into their business, Barbara recalls a marketing story that proved to be an ingenious success while bringing smiles to many faces: "Years ago, at an Interbike in Las Vegas, we produced a funny black T-shirt that stated on the front, 'I'd rather be riding an Italian,' and on the other side, Tommasini bikes. An incredible success! Tons of T-shirts sold out in a few minutes."

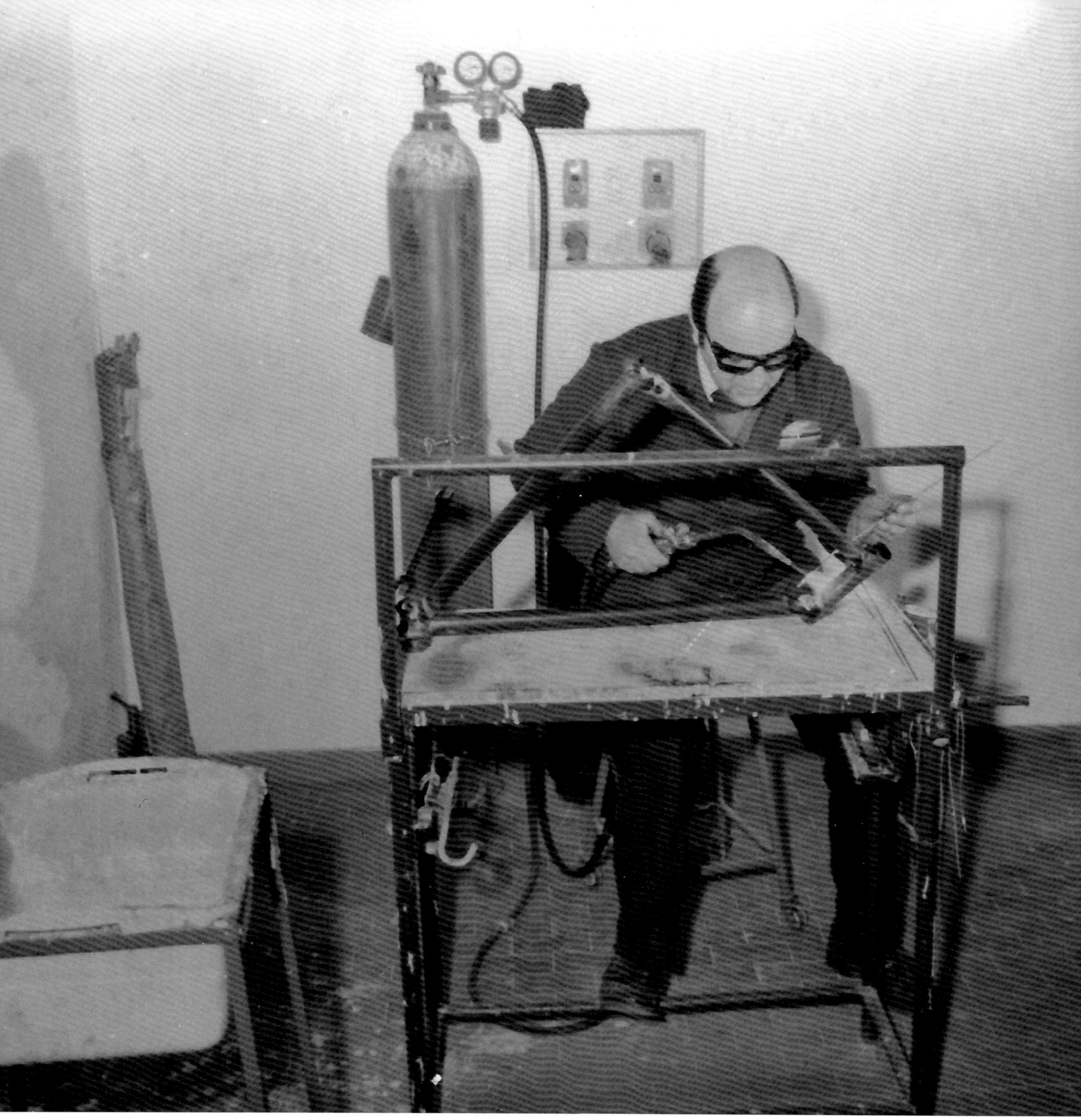

Irio Tommasini brazing a frame in his laboratory in 1975.
Courtesy of Tommasini family

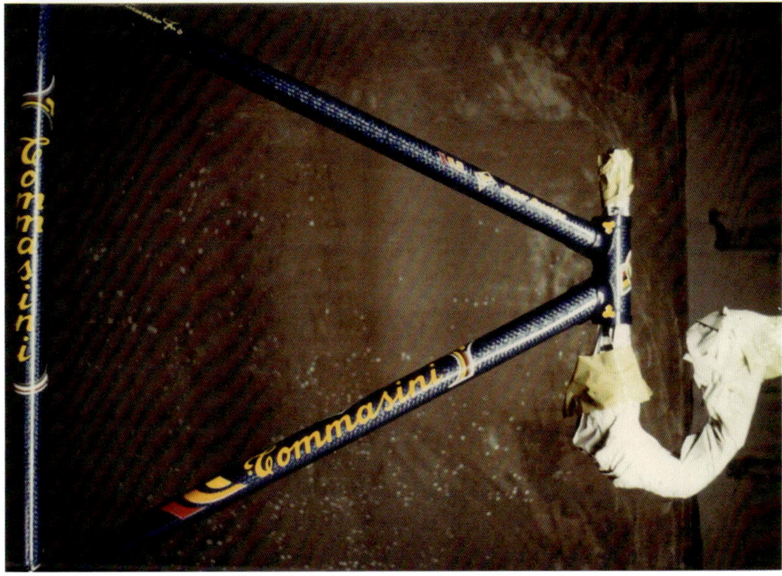

Original Retinato artwork and unique holographic designs from late 1982.
Courtesy of Tommasini family

Funny slogan used for T-shirts at Interbike 2007.
Courtesy of Barbara Tommasini

One of our happy customer's feedback pictures. *Courtesy of Tommasini*

The Tommasini family and "historical" staff of frame builders since the '70s at the Grifone Award, received from the town of Grosseto. This prize is awarded once a year to a single person or institution that was successfully recognized worldwide and made the town known as well. We received many awards like this among the years from different institutions. *Courtesy of Fotografia BF, Grosseto*

Roberta, the lady who traveled to meet us at the factory. A significant and inspiring bike moment. *Courtesy of Barbara Tommasini*

Detail of modern dropout, showing the attention to details and unique artwork we create at Tommasini. *Courtesy of Alessandro Baglioni*

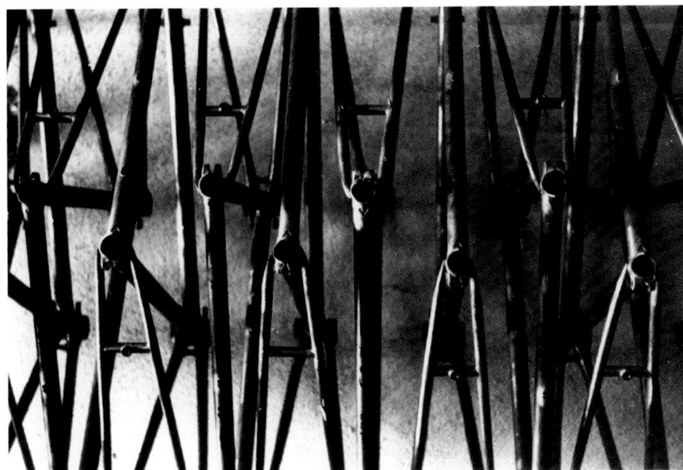

Raw frames. *Courtesy of Tommasini family*

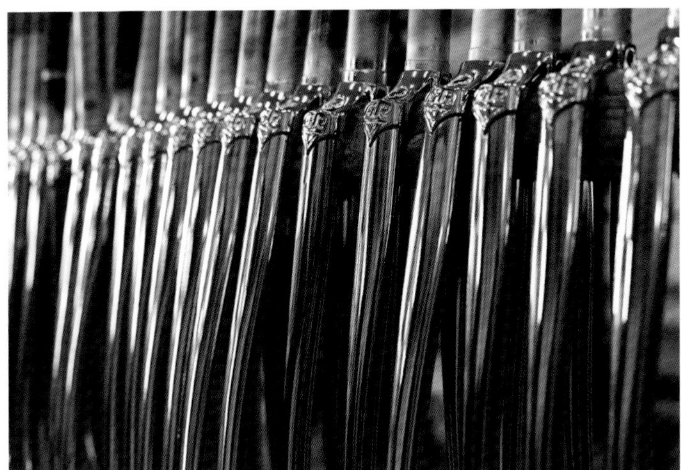

Tommasini air fork, a piece of art, a classic handmade fork that concentrates skills, excellent quality, and exquisite look. *Courtesy of Oliver Soulas*

SRAM 34T EAGLE TECHNOLOGY X-SYNC 2
EAGLE
GX
HUTCHINSON

WOODALPS

LUGRIN, FRANCE

In his professional life, Woodalps owner Arnaud Pornin is a mechanical engineer. Over the last few years, he's worked in the automobile and aeronautics industries and now works in the space sector on satellite structures and launcher components for a Swiss company. He was also on the French rowing team for several years and had it in mind to design and manufacture rowing boats during his studies. But he finally chose bikes.

One day, Arnaud set himself the challenge of building his own bike, after building a CNC (computerized numerical control) machining center: "I've always cycled as a hobby and as a means of transport." Being a specialist in composite materials, he could have gone for a carbon bike project, but with carbon, it was difficult to do something original with a limited budget. So, he chose wood. He says, "Wood, in particular ash, has a stiffness/mass ratio close to that of aluminum and allows great freedom of design. As I wanted to make an original bike that didn't look like the others, I decided to design a wooden bike." For ten years, he created and improved his bikes, and since they were so successful, he decided to market them.

When Arnaud started his Woodalps project, his workshop was a 6-square-meter ski storage room, so he had to dismantle his CNC machine to bring it in through the door. He says, "Now, I have a large, light-filled 90-square-meter workshop that allows me to work comfortably late at night. For creating his wooden bikes, Arnaud's favorite tool is his CNC milling machine:

A close-up view on the YGGO bike. *Courtesy of Woodalps*

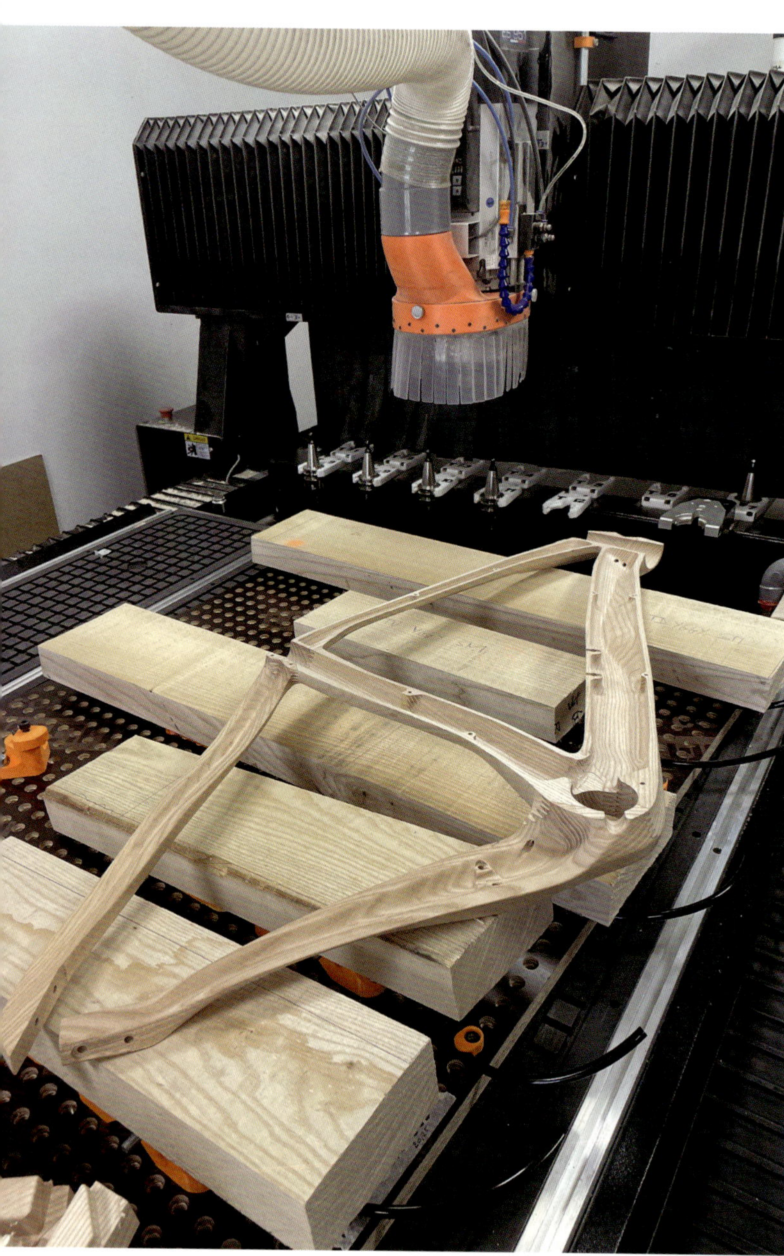

A half GROOTY frame on the CNC milling machine, at the beginning and at the end of machining operations. *Courtesy of Woodalps*

"But I also really like 3-D printing, which allows me to make lots of tools." Since he got his 3-D printer, he's printed over a thousand parts. "I print almost all my parts in orange, so there's a lot of orange in my workshop. Everything is designed in 3-D on the computer before being manufactured," he says.

Arnaud likes to create original things, adjusting shapes until he gets the right balance between performance and design: "In the design of Woodalps bikes, I try to put organic, dynamic shapes on each tube. None of the tubes on my bikes are simple cylindrical tubes. I also try to integrate the cables as much as possible, to obtain a clean result: The design process for a bike is long and complex. Each surface has a thickness adjusted to local stresses and impact exposure." When he starts a new bike, Arnaud says he looks for inspiration from concept bike sketches, trying to find some nice design features: "But in fact, the design I have implemented is simply linked to the objective to avoid all straight lines in the design."

Woodalps bikes attract a lot of attention, says Arnaud: "Even when you're riding on the road, cars will pull up to the same speed to look at the bike and say, 'Nice bike!' When the bike is parked in town, people crowd around it to look at it, touch it, and feel its weight by lifting it. When you're with your bike, a lot of people ask questions. It's definitely an original way to meet people!"

Arnaud says his bikes are totally influenced by his lifestyle: "The bikes I design are first and foremost made for me. I live in the Alps, on the shores of Lake Geneva. I mountain-bike every weekend, except in winter, when I ski. Soon, I'll be able to ride in winter because I'm working on a fat bike for riding on snow. I also like holidaying with my bikes. During the week, I ride my road bike a lot to get to work, which is 28 kilometers from home." Although Arnaud spends forty-three hours a week designing satellites and rocket components, he says, "My passion is bikes; it's more fun! Fortunately, I don't sleep much."

Shooting of the YGGY in my workshop. *Courtesy of Woodalps*

Me with a Branchy gravel frame in front of my CNC machine. *Courtesy of Woodalps*

My road bike, the GROOTY 4. *Courtesy of Woodalps*

The Branchy in front of The Dents du Midi in Switzerland. *Courtesy of Woodalps*

Opposite page:
My first gravel prototype. *Courtesy of Woodalps*

Amaury testing the YGGY in my playground, the mountains above Evian. *Courtesy of Woodalps*

The YGGY bike equipped with gravel tires. *Courtesy of Woodalps*

evian
COLU
MBUS

The YGGY during a bike trip in the Italian Dolomites.
Courtesy of Woodalps

Opposite: Maryline on the GROOTY during the Chatel Chablais Leman Race, on the climb to Col de Bassachaux. *Courtesy of Woodalps*

NOTES

1. Richard Hallett, *The Bike Deconstructed: A Grand Tour of the Modern Bicycle* (London: Princeton Architectural Press, 2014) (not paginated). For those interested in delving into the anatomy of a bicycle, there are numerous bicycle books available to suit the enthusiast through to someone with a casual interest.
2. Mario Manieri-Elia, *Louis H. Sullivan* (New York: Princeton Architectural Press, 1996), 60.
3. David McCullough, *The Wright Brothers* (London: Simon & Schuster, 2015), 22.
4. Alex Newton, *Bicycles That Changed the World* (London: Octopus, 2017), 14.
5. Tom Ambrose, *The History of Cycling in Fifty Bikes* (Crows Nest, Australia: Allen & Unwin, 2013), 68–69.
6. Ibid.
7. Ibid., 64.
8.Newton, *Bicycles That Changed the World*, 40.
9. "Art and Artists," MoMA, March 17, 2024, *https://www.moma.org/collection/works/88855*.
10. McCullough, *The Wright Brothers*, 22.
11. "Rare Craft Fellowship Award," American Craft Council, November 1, 2023, *https://www.craftcouncil.org/programs/past-programs/rare-craft-fellowship-award*.
12. "Our History," Calfee Design, December 28, 2023, https:/calfeedesign.com/start/about-us/.
13. Ibid.
14. Ibid.
15. Giles Belbin, "Tour de France History: Pélissier Ends 12-Year French Drought in 1923," *Cyclist*, January 11, 2023, *https://www.cyclist.co.uk/in-depth/tour-de-france-henri-pelissier*.

BIBLIOGRAPHY

Ambrose, Tom. *The History of Cycling in Fifty Bikes*. Crows Nest, Australia: Allen & Unwin, 2013.

American Craft Council. "Rare Craft Fellowship Award." Accessed November 1, 2023. *https://www.craftcouncil.org/programs/past-programs/rare-craft-fellowship-award*.

Belgin, Giles. "Tour de France History: Pélissier Ends 12-Year French Drought in 1923." *Cyclist*, January 11, 2023. https:/www.cyclist.co.uk/in-depth/tour-de-france-henri-pelissier.

Calfee Design. "Our History." Accessed December 28, 2024. *https://calfeedesign.com/start/about-us/*.

Hallett, Richard. *The Bike Deconstructed: A Grand Tour of the Modern Bicycle*. London: Princeton Architectural Press, 2014.

Manieri-Elia, Mario. *Louis H. Sullivan*. New York: Princeton Architectural Press, 1996.

McCullough, David. *The Wright Brothers*. London: Simon & Schuster, 2015.

MoMA. "Art and Artists." Accessed March 17, 2024. *https://www.moma.org/collection/works/88855*.

Newton, Alex. *Bicycles That Changed the World*. London: Octopus, 2017.

CONTACT DETAILS

The URLs listed here direct to the builders' web pages and are active at the time the book goes to print. If the websites have changed over time, please use a search engine to locate the new website of a given builder.

Acoustic Cycles
www.acousticcycles.com

Ahearne Cycles
www.ahearnecycles.com

Amapola Cycles
www.amapolacycles.com

Argonaut Cycles
www.argonautcycles.com

Atelier des Vélos
www.atelierdesvelos.com/en/home

Baum Cycles
www.baumcycles.com

BCB (Boucif Custom Bikes)
www.facebook.com/profile.php?id=100066794117906

Bilenky Cycle Works
https:/www.bilenky.com

Calfee Design
www.calfeedesign.com

Cycles Alex Singer
www.cycles-alex-singer.fr

Cycles Grand Bois
https:/cyclesgrandbois.com/index.html

Dario Pegoretti
https:/dariopegoretti.com

Ellis Cycles
www.elliscycles.com

Fern Bicycles
https:/www.fern-fahrraeder.de

Finnbar Trout Cycles
https:/finnbartroutcycles.com

Goodday Bikeworks
https:/www.gooddaycuriosity.com

Huhn Cycles
https:/huhncycles.com

ICHNU Cycles
https:/www.ichnu.com

Moulton Bicycle Company
https:/www.moultonbicycles.co.uk

Naked Bicycles and Design
https:/www.nakedbicycles.com

Parlee Cycles
https:/parleecycles.com

Prova Cycles
https:/www.provacycles.com

Quirk Cycles
https:/www.quirkcycles.com

Richard Sachs Cycles
https:/richardsachs.com

Rizzo Cycles
https:/rizzocycles.com

Scarab Cycles
https:/scarabcycles.com

Schön Studio
https:/www.schonstudio.com

SUEESS Frameworks
https:/www.sueess.bike

Sycip Designs
https:/www.sycip.com

TJ Cycles
https:/tjcycles.co.uk

Tommasini
https:/www.tommasini.com/en/

Woodalps
https:/www.woodalps.com/

ABOUT THE AUTHORS

Christine Elliott is an accomplished author and academic, having earned her PhD in book history from Monash University, Australia, in 2018. Her monograph *The Coffee-Table Book in the Post-war Anglophone World* was published in 2023. In 2008, she coauthored *Custom Bicycles: A Passionate Pursuit* with David Jablonka, which has achieved remarkable success with over 10,000 copies sold worldwide. Christine has enjoyed riding and cycling trips, including journeys from Venice to Florence in Italy and adventures in Greece. She lives in Victoria, Australia.

David Jablonka is a passionate cyclist with over 30 years of experience, including extensive rides in Australia, Europe, and the US. He coauthored *Custom Bicycles: A Passionate Pursuit* with Christine Elliott, a book that has sold over 10,000 copies globally. In addition to his cycling pursuits, David runs Second Chance Cycles, a community bike workshop in Collingwood, Melbourne, where he and a dedicated team recycle bicycles, teach bike mechanics, and provide bikes to those in need. He rides most days and actively participates in local cycling events such as Around the Bay in a Day and the Alpine Classic. He lives in Victoria, Australia.